Belle V

Manchester's Playground
Second Edition

Belle Vue sometime after 1949, when the old Jennison clock tower on the island had been demolished, and 1956, when construction of the Water Chute began. The goal posts for Belle Vue Rangers RUFC can be seen in the stadium.

Clive Hardy

iNostalgia

First published in 2005 by: First Edition Limited, 32 Stamford Street, Altrincham, Cheshire, WA14 1EY.

Second edition published in 2018 by: iNostalgia Ltd, Progress Centre, Charlton Place, Ardwick, Manchester M12 6HS.

Original Text 2005 edition by Heather Stackhouse and Daniel Hyams.

Text: © 2005 First Edition Limited.

Text: © 2018 second edition additional text Clive Hardy.

Images: © 2018 Jan Hollins, Manchester Evening News, Mirrorpix Limited.

Second edition design by Clive Hardy and Rick Preskey.

ISBN 978-1-84547-247-4

Belle Vue was the first UK venue David Cassidy played during his 1973 European tour.

Rise

For more than 150 years, Belle Vue was the entertainment centre for the North West in general and Manchester in particular. What started as a small zoological centre developed into a place of funfairs, firework displays, music, sports, boating lakes, greyhounds, beer and pies. At its height, it attracted two million people a year, with more than 170,000 recorded on one single day.

The park was famed for its innovations. The first greyhound meeting in the UK; the first speedway (dirt track motorcycle racing); one of the first stock car meetings; the country's largest bingo club; the country's largest teenage dance club; the first UK venue David Cassidy played.

Right up to the time of its sad and untimely demise, Belle Vue was a place which the people of the North West could be proud of – a fantasy destination just a bus ride away. So when, where, why did it all begin?

Belle Vue Zoological Gardens was the creation of John Jennison, a former silk weaver turned gardener with an interest in botany. When his father died in 1825, John inherited the family house which stood on a half-acre plot off Adswood Lane, Stockport. It was here, the following year, that he and his wife started their first venture; opening on summer Sunday afternoons selling garden produce. Within two or three years, Strawberry Gardens as it was then called, had become a full-time business for John. The addition of a small aviary, a brew house, and levying an admission charge, helped transform Strawberry Gardens into a successful business. By the mid-1830s it had outgrown its site.

Looking to expand, Jennison was advised to look at the Belle Vue area. In June 1836 he leased a disused lime pit for six months, though keeping Adswood in case things went pear-shaped. However, all went well, and Jennison signed a 99-year lease. Adswood was put up for sale but no buyer could be found, so it was leased out to a Mr Bramwell who ran it as a zoological garden. Alas, Bramwell failed to charge admission and the place became little more than a pub with a few cages of animals in its grounds.

Meanwhile, Belle Vue expanded so that by the mid-1840s the site included a gardens, some zoological exhibits such as monkeys and bears, and a small lake. With assistance from other members of the Jennison clan, further expansion included grottos, fountains, a maze and eventually individual themed gardens.

However, it had not been plain sailing. From the mid-1830s, some sectors of the UK economy were in difficulties. Though it was not a nationwide recession, the North West was hit. There were many reasons. A fall in the demand from Europe for British yarn and wool, and cotton trapped in a vicious spiral of over production, led to lower prices. But because mill owners had invested heavily in expensive equipment, they could not afford to reduce capacity to stabilise prices. On top of this, dozens of banks failed. The result was that Belle Vue began losing customers as they no longer had any spare cash to throw around.

In 1843, John Jennison himself was on the brink of going bust and some of his creditors wanted to force a sale of the site and get their money back.

BELLE VUE GARDENS MANCHESTER

OFFICIAL GUIDE — PRICE ONE PENNY

They also attempted to sell the old Adswood property but, like Jennison, failed to attract a buyer. Eventually, Jennison's creditors were persuaded to give him a chance to prove that his business idea was sound. It was. Thanks to an upturn in the economy, Jennison soon paid off his creditors in full. Jennison also attempted to revitalise Adswood by putting his son John in charge and stocking the place with spare animals from Belle Vue. Unfortunately, John lacked his father's business sense and the project was not a success. It was not until 1850 that Jennison senior was able to finally be legally separated from Adswood.

It was during 1843 that a lake was dug which included an island. Originally, the island was home to a natural history museum though this was moved in 1850 to rooms above the new aviary.

In 1851, after a visit to the Great Exhibition at the Crystal Palace, Hyde Park, Jennison returned enthused with ideas, including the beautiful and fantastic firework displays that Belle Vue became famous for. He also hired George Danson. As Belle Vue's scenic artist, Danson and his two sons would create 'theatre,' for the firework displays in the form of massive 30,000 square foot canvas backdrops. Jennison envisaged combining backdrop, dramatic fireworks and battle re-enactments from a major historical event into the sort of stuff to bring in the punters, 4,000 of which could be accommodated in a large elevated gallery. The actors in these extravaganzas were unemployed men from the local area who were paid mainly in beer and pies.

The first spectacular was *The Bombardment of Algiers*. The real event had taken place on 27 August 1816, when an Anglo-Dutch fleet under Admiral Lord Exmouth bombarded ships and harbour defences at Algiers to persuade the Dey of Algiers to release Christian slaves. The fleet fired 50,000 round shot, expending 118 tons of gunpowder and the bomb vessels fired 960 explosive mortar shells. The Dey ordered the release of 3,000 slaves.

The firework displays were crowd-pullers, though in 1859, Jennison got it completely wrong when the theme was *The Temple of Janus* – a firework display without a battle. At the time, the late Middle Ages poet, Durante degli Alighieri, better known as Dante, was very popular and considered to be one of the greatest of western Europe's poets. *The Temple of Janus* features in his work *The Divine Comedy*. Janus was the Roman god of

boundaries. The doors of his temple in Rome were closed in times of peace and open in times of war. Perhaps Belle Vue was trying to be too arty for its own good.

After Jennison died in 1867, his family continued his vision into the twentieth century. He had instilled in them a sense of self-sufficiency. Belle Vue made its own bricks, brewed its own beer, printed its own guides, made its own fireworks and grew its own vegetables.

By the time the nineteenth century was drawing to a close, Belle Vue was without doubt Manchester's premier attraction for the masses. The 1890 edition of Baedeker's guide to Great Britain states: 'Bellevue Gardens, Longsight, to the S.E., with zoological collection, dancing-saloon, restaurant, fire-works, lake for boating, etc., much frequented by the lower classes. They may be reached by tram or by train from London Road to Longsight.'

In 1925, the business was sold to Belle Vue (Manchester) Ltd and John Henry Iles was appointed managing director. Under Iles, the Gardens expanded to include a new amusement park. The following year, greyhound racing was introduced; it quickly became one of the most popular spectator sports of the interwar period. In 1928 the interior of the Kings Hall was remodelled so that it had a central stage area with seating for 5,000 circling round in tiers. It became the ideal venue for wrestling, boxing, music, and, from December 1929, the home of the Christmas Circus.

During 1928, speedway was tried out for the first time and Iles, quick to realise the crowd-pulling potential of this new spectator sport, oversaw the construction of a new stadium on a site next to the amusement park. The stadium was not solely designed for speedway. In the centre was a football pitch used by Belle Vue's short-lived professional football club, Manchester Central. The stadium was also used for political rallies, tennis tournaments, 500cc midget car racing and so on. From the 1950s, the speedway circuit itself was also used for stock car racing.

Belle Vue celebrated its centenary in 1936 with a redesign of some of the amusement park, gardens and zoo exhibits. The most well-known new feature was the floral clock with a statue of the Buddha placed on top. Behind the clock was a large Gibbon Cage and a new open-air exhibit called Monkey Mountain.

However, the Gibbon Cage and the Monkey Mountain were not a success. The moat around the Monkey Mountain was not wide enough to stop animals escaping, especially in winter when the water froze. The Gibbon Cage featured a house in the centre and it appears the gibbons were in the habit of attacking keepers who entered.

The Second World War proved a difficult time for Belle Vue. Although restrictions impacted on its activities, the park remained open for the duration, though areas were requisitioned for use by the military or for council allotments. The firework displays were cancelled and fair rides such as the Flying Sea Planes were closed. Ten rides were permitted to remain open.

The zoo became a refugee centre for animals evacuated from zoos forced to close. Unfortunately, those species reliant on food supplies from overseas suffered through lack of availability and many perished. It included the zoo's penguins who were wiped out through lack of fish and the sea lions who died from stomach ulcers after being fed beef soaked in cod-liver oil. Also, the entire collection of tropical fish died when the heating system failed due to a disruption in gas supplies. The monkeys were fed on boiled potatoes, and horse meat was allocated for animal consumption. However, the meat had to be marked with a harmless green dye and keepers wondered what the lions would make of it. Their ration was 8lb (3.6kg) of meat per lion per feed, and any hesitation was soon over.

One indirect casualty of the bombing was a bull bison killed by splinters from an anti-aircraft round. Splinters from anti-aircraft rounds also damaged the Reptile House, though as a precaution against animals escaping should the zoo be hit by bombs, keepers were armed with rifles. Then there was Gracie the hippo. She died on 3 December 1944, due to injuries inflicted by her mate Tony. Many animals have more acute hearing than humans and keepers reported that many showed signs of distress during air raids, even when the raids were some distance away. Given such evidence, the reintroduction of the firework spectacular in 1956 seems strange.

On a happier note, the Christmas Circus continued, though restricted to afternoon performances only. After the Free Trade Hall, Manchester, was bombed, the Halle Orchestra made the Kings Hall its home.

After the war, Belle Vue went through a boom period, especially at holiday weekends when crowds of 250,000 people were regular. Gerald Iles reinvigorated the zoo, gradually replacing species lost during the war. His radio programme, Children's Hour, increased in popularity and in 1951 he made his first TV appearance.

Belle Vue continued to inject a fun element into zoo exhibits – they would publicise feeding times for their animals, with the hippos and sealions firm favourites. On the down side, the zoo suffered bouts of vandalism and burglary, resulting in the death or disappearance of animals. In April 1960, keepers discovered that the zoo had been broken in to and 38 birds killed, including nine penguins.

However, the immediate post-war boom had come to an end by 1951 and attendances had started to decline. The Company invested to stop the rot. The year 1954 saw the first staging of a firework spectacular in the old Jennison mould since the 1930s. The same year Stock Car Racing was introduced and proved a hit with the crowd.

John Jennison (right) exploring the Indian Temple and Grotto.

The last grand Jennison-style firework display took place in 1956 – the theme was Robin Hood and his Merrie Men. It was not a financial success and subsequent displays were scaled down.

By now the company was in financial difficulties due to a combination of high taxation, falling attendances and continued post-war restrictions on building work. An approach was made to Sir Leslie Joseph – a man with a wealth of experience in the amusement business - and his partner Charles Forte. It resulted in the appointment of Sir Leslie as Managing Director, and Charles Forte as Deputy Chairman. H F B Iles continued in his post as Chairman, and others who retained their posts included Gerald Iles and Johnnie Hoskins.

Redevelopment was the order of the day. Work began on a new major ride – the Water Chute. The miniature railway was rerouted to run between the Ballroom and the Great Lake. Louis Tussaud's Waxworks opened as did the Enchanted Garden with its elevated walkway.

Under the influence of Charles Forte, catering facilities expanded. Dining out in the 1950s was a novel experience for many. The extent of most pubs' menus ran to ham, or cheese and onion sandwiches, though the dreaded chicken in the basket would soon make its appearance.

In October 1957, Belle Vue opened the first of its themed catering outlets – the Bavarian Banqueting Suite. Others followed. The Cumberland and Windermere Suites were the result of the rebuilding of the old Belfast and Exhibition Hall Restaurants, and an extension added to the Palm Court.

In 1958 the park suffered a serious fire. The Pagoda Restaurant was destroyed as were the Tudor Suite, the York and American bars, the Baronial Hall, the Popular Café, five shops, the outdoor dancing platform, the fireworks viewing platform and the staff canteen. The fire also threatened some of the zoo's animals but due to the quick response from firemen and staff alike, most of the animals were saved. One casualty was a 17-year-old lioness named Judy, who became so distressed that she had to be put down.

During 1963 there was another takeover. Charles Forte gained control and from then onwards Belle Vue became a subsidiary of the Forte Holding Company. The new owners invested and improvements to the zoo continued, though Forte still concentrated on developing the dining and exhibition halls. In October 1964, fire broke out in the northwest corner of the complex close to the speedway stadium, engulfing the Cumberland and Windemere Suites. Four fire appliances were soon on the scene and as their crews tackled the blaze, the decision was taken to evacuate 3,000 bingo players from the Kings Hall. Some damage was done to the speedway stadium though, within a year, it and the suites were all were functioning again. During rebuilding, the company added a new Kendal Suite.

The 1960s also saw the opening of the Miniland model village and completion of the Tropical River House, where Hercules the hippo gained a reputation for eating some of his fellow inmates. The roof of the Central Exhibition Hall was raised enabling the venue to stage boat shows. However, during the 1970s, Belle Vue would once again face financial pressures.

One of the many official guides produced for visitors. The first guide was printed in 1847 and featured a splendid artist's layout detailing numerous attractions that at the time included a racecourse, a Maze on the Kirkmanshulme Lane side of the gardens, small lake, and a zoological collection.

From 1881 to 1894, the books included a simple layout plan, but this was dropped from the 1895 edition in favour of a bird's eye view engraving on which attractions were individually numbered. This was also the first edition to contain coloured illustrations. The bird's eye view engraving was used for 30 years by which time it was out of date.

The 1957 edition featured the early redevelopment carried out by Sir Leslie Joseph and Charles Forte, including the Enchanted Forest, Elevated Tree Walk, and the Water Chute.

Sixteen years later, the guide depicted a car park where the Boating Lake had once been; the Belle Vue Granada Bowl; a cartoon cinema and the zoo in its final form.

An external and internal photographs of Belle Vue Gaol. Owned by Manchester Corporation, the prison was built on Hyde Road, West Gorton in 1848. There were four sections to the prison, three for male prisoners and one for female. The jail was not a capital sentence prison, its inmates usually given short-term sentences of no more than six months. However, there were a few prisoners – mainly deserters from the army - who were sent there for periods of up to two years.

Even so, the gaol's claim to fame came in the 'Manchester Outrage' of 1867. Two men, Thomas J Kelly and Timothy Deasy, had been arrested under the vagrancy act and along with four other inmates were being taken by prison van to court in Manchester. However, the pair were anything but vagrants – they were Fenians – members of the Irish Republican Brotherhood. As the van passed under a railway bridge on Hyde Road, it was attacked by 30-40 men – some were armed. The van's mounted escort fled. Inside the van and carrying the keys to the prisoners' shackles was City of Manchester Police sergeant Charles Brett, who was shot and killed after the van's doors had been blown with explosives. The two men escaped. Five men were eventually arrested. William Allen, Michael Larkin, Michael O'Brien, Thomas Maguire and Edward O'Meagher Condon, stood trial for murder. Allen, Larkin and O'Brien were hanged in public at Salford Gaol on 23 November 1867. The death sentences on the other two were overturned. Sergeant Charles Brett was the first city police officer to be killed in the line of duty.

This excitement apart, inmates and warders alike could hear the dramatic Belle Vue firework displays and even the howls of some of the zoo's inmates. In 1877 the prison passed into Government control but 11 years later was declared unsafe due to damage to the foundations caused by local mining operations. It was finally demolished in 1890, Strangeways becoming Manchester's principal prison.

Some of the recovered building blocks were bought by Jennison and used during the construction of the rhino enclosure. The above image shows how close the prison was to Jennison's Belle Vue Gardens.

Flat caps and bowler hats for the men and straw boaters for the girls! This 1900 photograph shows the open-air dancing area with the Lighthouse Café on the left of the picture. On the right is a large painted backdrop used during one of the fantastic firework spectaculars.

Some of the cast for one of the firework spectaculars. Rails were added to the firework island in 1856. This enabled heavy scenery to be attached to one of ten rail-mounted trucks, allowing it to be moved around as required during performances.

From the same firework spectacular. A closer look at the "ladies" on the rail-mounted mobile contraption reveals the stiff collars, ties and masculine faces of at least three of the guys from the previous image.

In 1887, Colonel William F Cody, better known as Buffalo Bill, brought his Wild West show to the UK for the first time to coincide with the American Exhibition in London. When the exhibition ended, Buffalo Bill took his show to the provinces and in the November set up on the banks of the Irwell in Salford, on the site now occupied by the Lowry Gallery.

The show was a great success and for five months played to packed houses. Cody again toured the UK during 1891-92, shortly after several Native American tribes had made one last bid for freedom during the time of the Ghost Dances.

In 1903, Cody returned to the North West. With him were 97 First Nation Americans – mainly Lakota and Oglala Sioux, Cheyenne and Pawnees. Also appearing were the sharpshooters Annie Oakley and Lilian Smith as well as the likes of Buck Taylor (King of the Cowboys), and Richard Johnson (The Giant Cowboy). Spectators were treated to a series of Native American attacks against a wagon train, a stagecoach and a settler's hut – all of which were beaten off by Buffalo Bill and his scouts.

Our image shows Cody (standing on the tram's staircase) and the First Nation members of his show on a visit to Belle Vue. When the show pulled out of town, a Lakota chief by the name of Charging Thunder (pictured below) decided to remain in Salford. He married Josephine, one of the show's horse trainers, and settled down in Darwen, moving later to West Gorton. Charging Thunder changed his name to George Edward Williams and did a variety of jobs including working as a doorman at the Central Cinema, Clewes Street, near Belle Vue. He also worked at Belle Vue looking after the elephants and might have appeared in the first circus in 1922.

A family story is that when Charging Thunder had had too much to drink, he would head for the elephant house to sleep it off. It was said that his favourite elephant, Nellie, would stand watch over him.

Charging Thunder died of pneumonia in 1929, aged 52. He is buried in Gorton Cemetery.

(Opposite page top). Charles and Richard Jennison standing before the Indian Temple and Grotto in 1906. Charles spent most of his time overseeing the botanical aspects of the gardens, while Richard was more comfortable looking after the many visitors that flocked to Belle Vue. Richard was the last of the brothers and when he died aged 82 in 1919, sole ownership of the zoo passed to the third generation of the family

(This page). The Chinese Café was incredibly popular with visitors. The brightly coloured Chinese lanterns, parasols and painted walls were in stark relief against the starched Victorian dress of the waitresses. The Jennisons originally decorated the café in this fashion in 1889 and it remained in this style for many years.

(Opposite page bottom). There were many events held at Belle Vue over the years, including the dog show featured in this image. The first conformation Dog Show was held in the Town Hall at Newcastle-upon-Tyne in 1859, and over the following decade or so, popularity for such events increased dramatically. The Kennel Club was formed in 1873 and published its first Stud Book in 1874. It listed all Dog Show results since 1859 and laid down the rules for running shows and field trials. From 1880, the club published a monthly register of dogs in the *Kennel Gazette* and these records have gone on to become a major source for pedigree information.

In 1890, the first edition of the *Our Dogs* newspaper was published in Manchester and continues to this day. Manchester was also home to the first mass-produced tinned dog food in the UK. The Chappell Brothers factory at Pendleton produced Ken-L-Ration until the mid-1930s when the company was acquired by Mars Foods. They soon moved production to Slough and changed the product name to Chappie – it would later be rebranded as Pedigree Chum.

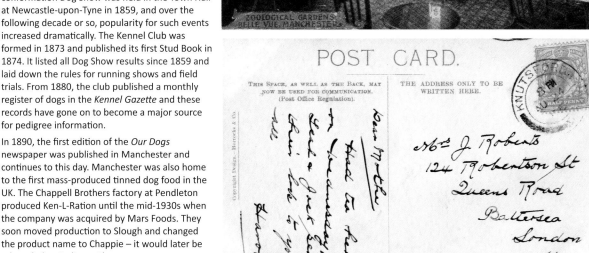

(Opposite page top). Standing to attention in front of the firework viewing platform is the recently formed 19th (Service) Battalion (4th City Pals) of the Manchester Regiment. On 28th August 1914, the Manchester Regiment was authorised to raise four Pals battalions. Recruiting for the 19th commenced on 2 September 1914, and two weeks later the battalions were at full strength.

(Opposite page bottom). During the World War Two, many of Belle Vue's grounds and buildings were requisitioned for use by the military. Pictured here are two factory girls being shown a Bren gun mounted on a tripod, so it could be used as an anti-aircraft weapon.

(This page). During the Queen's visit to Lancashire in May 1961, she presented new guidons (colours) to the Duke of Lancaster's Own Yeomanry. One of the monarch's titles is the Duke of Lancaster, making Queen Elizabeth the Honorary Colonel of the Regiment.

Manchester-born David Lloyd George addresses a huge crowd at Belle Vue in 1924. He was less than two-years-old when his mother was widowed and moved the family to live with her brother in Wales. Lloyd George joined the Liberal Party and became an MP in 1890. He was Prime Minister of a coalition government during the Great War.

Probably the best orator in England in the 1930s, Sir Oswald Mosley (on the right), 6th Baronet of Ancoats, arriving at Manchester for a speech at Belle Vue. He was Member of Parliament for Harrow from 1918-1924, and for Smethwick from 1926-31.

As Chancellor of the Duchy of Lancaster (1929-31), Mosley was one of Labour's more able members. He proposed bringing down mass unemployment by putting money into public works programmes, raising the school leaving age by one year, and introducing liveable pensions. He also advocated the introduction of credit controls. Instead, the Government stuck to its draconian unemployment policies.

Mosley resigned, and the following day formed the New Party along with six Labour MPs who had signed the Mosley Manifesto, though two of them quickly resigned and sat as independents. In the 1931 Ashton-under-Lyne by-election, New Party candidate Allan Young split the left-wing vote allowing the Conservative candidate to take the seat. The New Party fielded 25 candidates for the 1931 General Election but failed to return a member.

In the early days, the New Party was popular. It received a £50,000 donation from Lord Nuffield and had many admirers including Aneurin Bevan and Harold MacMillan. However, during 1932 the New Party morphed into the British Union of Fascists, remembered these days for Mosley's bodyguard, the blackshirts.

At its height, the BUF had a mass following and is thought to have had around 50,000 members. However, its increasingly radical and anti-Semitic stance alienated many followers. For others, the final straw came at a BUF rally at Olympia in June 1934, when the violence initiated by the blackshirts finally cost the party what remained of its support from the popular press.

Doreen Sawyer, Secretary of the Eules (Lanes) Branch of the League of Youth, and Herbert Morrison at a Labour Rally at Belle Vue in November 1951.

Herbert Morrison was one of the leading lights behind the 1951 Festival of Britain. On a budget of £12million (about £391million in 2018) and with little support from the Conservatives, the festival to showcase to the world the very latest in British scientific, engineering, technological, architectural and artistic achievements proved a resounding success.

Morrison was made Foreign Secretary following the resignation of Ernest Bevin. However, he was not in the job for long as Labour lost the 1951 General Election despite polling more votes than the Tories. He retired from the Commons following Labour's defeat in the 1955 General Election.

(Bottom). Ken Dodd, North West Labour Princess Sandra Farmer, and Harold Wilson, at the North West Festival of Labour at Belle Vue in July 1962.

The stage set for the first post-war firework spectacular, *The Storming of Quebec*. It was staged in 1954 following the lifting of wartime building controls. During the war, the Defence Regulations had restricted private building work unless carried out with approval from a Government Department, or with a licence from the Ministry of Works. Some regulations were carried over into peace time to prohibit the use of materials on unnecessary building work – even repairs. The costs of staging these spectaculars had rocketed since the 1930s. Each involved months of preparation, costly scenery, and several hundred extras who now wanted cash rather than pies and pints.

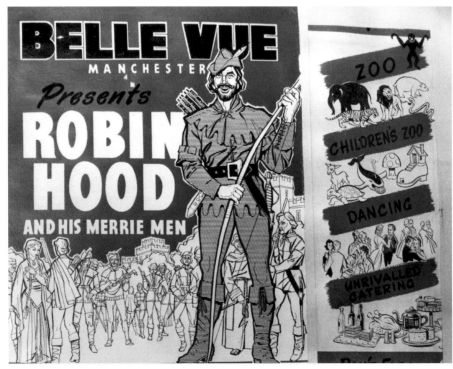

Publicity poster for what turned out to be the third and final post-war firework spectacular, *Robin Hood and his Merrie Men*, which was staged in 1956. At the time, one of ATV Television's hit shows was *The Adventures of Robin Hood*, starring Richard Greene in the title role. The spectacular was not a financial success. From 1957, until the last display in 1969, it would be fireworks only.

Fireworks of a different kind. In the early hours of 17 January 1958, a fire broke out in the Great Ballroom. Spreading quickly, it engulfed the Pagoda and York Restaurants, the Gallery Bar and staff canteen. It also destroyed the office of Belle Vue's resident musical director Fred Bonelli, consigning more than 5,000 music scores to the flames, as well as the studio of Syd Lane, Belle Vue's commercial artist and set designer.

The 240ft long Parrot/Lion House was also threatened. Head keeper Matt Kelly arrived on the scene still clad in his pyjamas and bedroom slippers. Even so, he began the evacuation of the Parrot House whilst zoo superintendent Mr Wilson took charge of the big cats. One of the lionesses, Judy, became so distressed that she had to be put down. With flames rising 60-70ft in the air, there was the distinct possibility that the big cats might be lost should the flames spread.

The bottom image, taken at daybreak, shows the still smouldering remains of the York Restaurant and Coronation Ballroom.

LION HOUSE

PAGODA RESTAURANT

GALLERY BAR

STAFF CANTEEN

The fire came close to engulfing the Lion House. Armed police were deployed to shoot animals should it become necessary. However, firefighters saved it by using every available hose to cover the building with a tunnel of water. The damage was estimated at £250,000 (about £5.75million in 2018).

It is 1964 and fire strikes again. Tangled metal and charred woodwork mark what were once the Cumberland and Windermere Suites.

The remains of the entrance to the Cumberland and Windermere Suites.

In October 1978, fire again ravaged the banqueting suites. The suites had space for storage and among the items destroyed were valuable circus equipment, and the coconut matting used in the Kings Hall.

Daily Mirror Day at Belle Vue, 11 June 1962. As can be seen, the Mirror's page one lead is that a further 52 soldiers serving with the British Army of the Rhine (BAOR) were to be tried by courts martial for 'civil crimes' rather than against Army discipline. The announcement came within a week of the revelation that six soldiers serving with the Lancashire Regiment had been jailed in March, after being tried in secret by courts martial on charges relating to a brawl in an Army canteen. Another revelation was that 21 soldiers serving with the Cameronians had been sentenced to detention – 19 for a café brawl, two for theft and causing damage.

(Opposite page, top left). Talent show time at the *Daily Mirror Day* at Belle Vue, Whitsun 1962. (Opposite page, top right). Winner of the Mr Beefcake competition. Daily Mirror Day at Belle Vue, Whitsun 1962. (Opposite page, bottom). Fashion contest. *Daily Mirror Day* at Belle Vue, Whitsun 1962.

By the end of the 1950s, the UK was in the grip of bingo mania, with sessions being held in pubs, clubs, cinemas and dance halls. Not to be left out, Belle Vue started what its publicity department described as the "largest bingo club in the Country." By September 1961, twice-weekly sessions were being held in the Kings Hall, attracting nightly attendances of between 3,500-4,000 players. Sessions were held on Friday and Sunday nights, though our image from August 1963 was taken during an open-air event. For Belle Vue, the love affair with bingo was relatively short-lived. Attendances declined, and the Friday night session was abandoned during 1964. The Sunday session continued into 1966.

(Right) In this publicity shot from December 1969, Sam Mason, the landlord of Caesar's Palace, arrives in the chariot hauled by circus girls Sandra Ashley (left) and Sue Neilson. Caesar's Palace was at the Hyde Road entrance and had already been through several incarnations; public house, restaurant, hotel. The conversion to Caesar's Palace took place in 1969, with the main bar decorated in the style of Ancient Rome.

The conversion did not last as long as the Western Roman Empire and this particular Rome fell in 1976. The place was then remodelled as Jennison's Ale House. The chariot used in this image was from the Samson and Delilah act at the circus. Samson, alias strong man Trevor Barnett, is standing on the steps. Disaster struck the building in August 1980, when the front parapet gave way and collapsed on to the forecourt. A survey revealed that the building was structurally unsafe, leading to its immediate closure and demolition.

(Opposite page bottom) *Daily Mirror* stand at a trade exhibition for newsagents.

Opened in 1876, the Lake Hotel, Belle Vue, was situated on the junction of Hyde Road, Mount Road and Kirkmanshulme Lane. A local landmark, it was eventually destroyed by fire. Our image dates from 1971.

The Hyde Road entrance, complete with model triceratops. The Palm Court Bar and original entrance are in the background.

The Zoo

By 1856 the Jennison family had added lions, rhinos, bears, gazelles and kangaroos to their collection at Belle Vue. In 1860 they acquired an elephant from Ceylon which was named Sally. Twelve years later, the Jennisons paid £680 (£76,160.00 at 2018 prices) for an Asian elephant at an auction in Edinburgh. The elephant, named Maharaja, was supposed to come to Manchester by train but as they attempted to load him into a van attached to the 10.05am express, Maharaja panicked and wrecked the vehicle. Calm was restored when an unemployed lion tamer, Lorenzo Lawrence, stepped forward to help. Maharaja quietened down and Lorenzo was hired to bring him to Manchester – on foot. The pair covered 28 miles a day. Maharaja lived at Belle Vue for ten years giving rides to children and dying at the age of 18. Lorenzo remained at Belle Vue for more than 40 years.

The zoo continued to expand. An Elephant House was built in 1873, though it was replaced by a larger building in 1876, the same year the Lion House was enlarged and the first hippopotamus arrived. Her entry is T29 in the common hippo studbook, though no name is recorded. The first Penguin House was erected in 1888 and comprised a 40ft (12.19metres) glass tank and, before the century was over, an open-air sealion pool had been added.

In 1925, control of Belle Vue passed to Belle Vue (Manchester) Ltd. During the early years of the new company, investment in the zoo declined and it was not until the appointment of Gerald Iles as Zoological Superintendent that its fortunes were reversed. Having just finished a zoology degree at Manchester University, Iles willingly took up the challenge to turn the zoo around.

Funds were made available to Iles to upgrade the zoo in time for the 1936 Centenary celebrations. The Elephant House was remodelled, the Reptile House was extended and modernised and new exhibits such as the Monkey Mountain and the Gibbon Cage added.

Though the zoo remained open during the Second World War, Iles had only a skeleton crew left to help him. The zoo also became a refuge for animals evacuated from zoos forced to close. It was not easy. By 1940, food supplies were becoming problematic for some species and many died including all the penguins.

In 1946, Iles had a new Head Keeper, Matt Kelly, who took over from James Craythorne. Kelly worked closely with Iles and the pair would be recognised for their dedication in ensuring Belle Vue's reputation for quality.

Gerald Iles finally said goodbye to Belle Vue in October 1957 to take up a post in Montreal, Canada. His place was taken by William Wilson, whose claim to fame was to build adobe huts resembling a Mexican village as sleeping quarters for the Ankole Watusi cattle and the zebras. Wilson's tenure as zoo superintendent was short. He was relieved of his position in 1961 and Matt Kelly took over until a suitable replacement could be found.

Raymond Legge, who had spent time as superintendent at both Chester and Blackpool zoos, came to Belle Vue in 1962. Legge was very much in the Iles mould. During his first year, a new Penguin House was completed and the following year he displayed a talent for the Gerald Iles style of showmanship, when he introduced the Chimps' Tea Party. In 1963, Legge oversaw improvements to the giraffe enclosure and a new ostrich and emu paddock. Work also began on a new Great Ape House.

One of the outstanding developments of the mid-1960s was a new Aquarium and Reptile House. Both were divided into three sections; the Aquarium into British native species; fish from coral reefs, and tropical freshwater species. The Reptile House featured an area landscaped to represent a tropical rain forest, complete with alligators, crocodiles and turtles. In 1965, a female American alligator laid eggs. Had they hatched out, Belle Vue would have been the first zoo in Europe to breed this species in captivity. The other sections housed snakes and lizards. In zoological terms, Belle Vue finally achieved a European first in 1972 when a Royal Python gave birth.

Belle Vue's last superintendent, Peter Grayson, took over from Raymond Legge in 1971. By then the owners appeared reluctant to invest in the zoo and closure suddenly seemed imminent, though it would be another six years before the fateful announcement would be made.

In June 1893, the Jennisons bought a chimpanzee called Consul from one of Wombwell's travelling menageries that was being dispersed in London. Friendly and not aggressive, Consul was to be seen around Belle Vue wearing a striped blazer and hat, drinking beer and smoking a clay pipe. Alas he died just over a year later. Such was his popularity with the public that the Jennison family attempted to keep Consul's death a secret - even to the extent of acquiring a doppelganger. However, the new Consul was soon rumbled as he was aggressive. Quickly renamed Consul II, he is pictured performing his party trick - playing a violin whilst riding a tricycle. Later, he progressed to riding a bicycle.

The image below was taken in July 1975, when Topaz the chimp was still quite young. She is pictured raising a finger to her lips to let her keeper know she is hungry.

By 1976, Topaz had become a fruit machine addict. It started when her keeper took her for a stroll around the amusement arcade and let her pull the lever a time or two. After that, Topaz pestered her keeper every day to take her to play the one-armed bandit. If she won, her keeper kept the winnings and Topaz received an extra helping of bananas and raisins.

Ten-day-old Penny the pigtailed macaque gets up close and personal with the *MEN* photographer.

Blanco was just one day old when his mother deserted him. So, zoo superintendent Peter Grayson stepped in, took the baby lion home and hand-reared him. This image was taken in May 1976 when Blanco was 18 months old. Grayson would take Blanco on regular walks around the zoo and sometimes even took him for a stroll along Hyde Road. Because he was hand-reared, it was considered unsafe for Blanco to return to the main lion enclosure.

Blanca was also deserted by her mother but had an unusual surrogate family of Afghan hounds. The Tait family and their Afghans reared Blanca until she was old enough to return to Belle Vue.

One of the trio of cubs born to Jason and Sally in the late 1970s. When the zoo closed, most of the lions were moved to Cleethorpes, though one of the cubs went to Knaresborough.

John Cristy was head keeper at the time of the zoo's closure. He is pictured here with one of the lion cubs.

(Top right). Rita the tigon was purchased from Vincennes Zoo, Paris, in July 1957, when she was six years old. She was the zoo's third tigon and lived until February 1968. (Above). Over the years, the zoo owned three tigons – the result of a male tiger mating with a lioness. The first two, a brother and sister, were bought from Dresden Zoo in 1936. Kliou and Maude's parents were a Manchurian tiger and an African lioness. The siblings did not get on and had to be separated. Kliou died in 1941, his sister in 1949.

Peter Grayson with Topaz the chimpanzee and Luke the leopard.

Children are treated to free elephant rides during *Daily Mirror Day*, Whitsun 1962.

For decades, elephant rides were a popular attraction at Belle Vue. In 1921 an Indian elephant named Lil arrived at the zoo with her keeper Phil Fernandez. Phil was originally from Malaysia and when he accompanied elephants that were giving rides, he would dress in flamboyant Indian robes.

For around six decades, Belle Vue's elephants earned their keep not only giving rides to visitors, but also doing general haulage work around the gardens and providing power for the coffee-grinding mill. They also took part in some of the firework spectaculars and helped with demolition work. The visitor rides ended in the 1960s.

Tensing the kitten meets Moti and Kali, two young Asiatic elephants. The image shows the remodelled stalls dating from the 1930s.

(Below). In 2018 this is the stuff of health and safety nightmares, but back in February 1965 it seemed perfectly normal put little Lisa Roland in with Belle Vue's new arrived baby elephant. Both were 13 months old, so what could possibly go wrong? Thankfully nothing did.

(Bottom). Originally, the elephants were housed individually in cramped stalls, but during the mid-1930s the Elephant House was remodelled to give each animal more room. The individual stalls were redesigned so that each could take two animals and still offer space to move around. Outside, the iron and oak paddock fencing was replaced with short spikes and a moat. In the 1960s, a larger outdoor paddock was added.

When Belle Vue's elephants were sold, Twiggy went to Amersfoort Zoo, Amsterdam, arriving there on 30 November 1977. On 15 October 1990 she moved to Belgrade Zoo, where, as of 1 January 2015, she was still alive and well.

Peter Grayson and chums.

(Top and middle). Matt (left) and Daisy, were the zoo's pygmy hippos. Pygmy hippos can have a lifespan of 30-40 years in the wild and have been known to live for up to 55 years in captivity. They stand 2.46–3.38ft at the shoulder (75-100cm), are 4.92-5.74ft (150-175cm) long and generally weigh in at between 300-606 pounds (136-275kg). Their bodies are greenish black or brown in colour and almost completely hairless and they secrete the same clear mucus as common hippos to keep their skin moist. The mucus is thought to have antiseptic and sun-screening properties. Native to the forests and swamps of West Africa, they are nocturnal herbivores that spend much of their time in water. When born, pygmy hippos cannot swim and have to be taught.

According to the pygmy hippo international studbook, Matt (number 276) was born at Washington Zoo on 15 December 1968 and arrived at Belle Vue on 17 February 1970. Daisy (number 397) was caught in the wild, arriving at Belle Vue on 1 January 1970. She had her first calf with Matt on 1 February 1975, but it died. On 5 October 1976, she gave birth to Maisie (number 458).

When Belle Vue closed, Matt, Daisy, and Maisie, were sold to Bristol Zoo, where they arrived on 3 October 1977. For the first time, Bristol Zoo had a proven breeding herd of pygmy hippos. At Bristol, Daisy gave birth to three more calves of which only the third, Julie, survived. Julie was Bristol's first successful pygmy hippo birth. Matt died on 17 November 1985 and Daisy on 26 January 1990.

(Bottom). Common hippos, Nicholas and dad Tony work the crowd, tempting visitors to throw them the odd sandwich, or loaf, or anything else edible. Tony had been caught wild in the Sudan, arriving at Belle Vue during February 1930. Nicholas' mother was Gracie. She was three years younger than Tony and had been born in captivity at Amsterdam Zoo on 26 October 1930. She arrived at Belle Vue on 3 June 1937. Gracie died on 3 December 1944, from injuries inflicted by her mate Tony.

The first mention of a hippo at Belle Vue is a brief entry for number T29 in the common hippo studbook. It was female and arrived from an unknown source during 1876 and died in 1905. The next entry is number T62, a male, born at Amsterdam Zoo on 30 October 1906. It was moved to Hannover Zoo on 22 July 1907, arriving at Belle Vue on 24 June 1908. It died in 1930.

On 16 May 1964, Belle Vue took delivery of Fifi from Whipsnade Zoo. She had been born in captivity at Paris Zoo on 11 April 1953, moving to London Zoo on 30 August 1957. From there, Fifi went to Whipsnade on 1 October 1960. Fifi died at Belle Vue in 1977. She was mated with Nicholas and gave birth on 4 January 1965, but the calf died the same day.

Nicholas the hippo about to enjoy a cake brought for him by some children from Birmingham. June 1960. Despite the smile, hippos, are notoriously unpredictable and highly aggressive. They usually weigh in at 2,870-3,310 pounds (1,300-1,500kg) and can live 40-50 years, though the oldest to die in captivity was Donna at the Mesker Park Zoo, Indiana, who was 61 when she passed away. Nicholas was born at Belle Vue on 5 December 1938 and died on 11 May 1965.

According to vet David Taylor's book, Zoo Vet, Hercules the hippo was born at Whipsnade, though Hercules is first mentioned in the common hippo studbook as arriving at Belle Vue in February 1965 from Humberside (Cleethorpes Zoo?). Hercules was sold to Cleethorpes in 1977 where he was a star attraction. Opened in 1965 it closed shortly after Hercules arrived. It was soon reopened by Colossus Ltd but closed permanently a couple of years later. Hercules was on the move again, this time to Dudley Zoo, where he died of peritonitis on 16 November 1979.

There is a story that when Belle Vue opened the Tropical River House, Hercules found a new hobby whereby he would stalk, kill and eat some of the other residents – mainly tropical birds.

Addie the giraffe looks in on the zoo's latest arrival, a baby zebra born on cup final day 1973 and named after Sunderland's goalkeeper Jim Montgomery. Second Division Sunderland were taking on cup-holders Leeds United. Jim became Sunderland's man of the day when he pulled off a superb double save – a header from Trevor Cherry, then a shot from Peter Lorimer that prevented Leeds from equalising and gave Sunderland the cup. At the end of the match, Sunderland manager Bob Stokoe ran on to the pitch and embraced Jim. An act commemorated to this day by a statue outside the Stadium of Light.

A group of zebras is called a dazzle, and the latest addition to Belle Vue's dazzle was Zeek. Superintendent Peter Grayson introduces Zeek to some of the children from Richmond Infants School, Oldham, who had picked Zeek's name for him.

(Above right). Recent additions to the zoo in June 1952 included the Ankole Watusi calf Sitatunga (pictured at right). New-born calves weigh 31-51 pounds (14–23 kg), adult cows 948-1,190 pounds (430–540 kg) and bulls 1,190-1,609 pounds (540–730 kg). Sitatunga has yet to grow her horns. As an adult, the horns can reach 8ft (244cm) between the tips. The horns act as a radiator, circulating and cooling the blood before returning it to the body of the animal.

(Above left). New-born camel and mum.

(Below). A familiar sight during the late 1930s were the llama rides.

Giraffes, George and Mary get friendly with the visitors in this image taken during 1936. Though giraffes had been a part of the zoo since 1871, it was not until 1937 that a calf was born at Belle Vue, when Mary gave birth to Doreen.

Youki the giraffe gives a motherly lick to two new arrivals, muscovite ducklings, being taken round the zoo by Angela Melia (19), on the left, and Eileen Simkiss (16).

The kitten and the cockatoo. May 1962.

(Right). Janette Sparrow, aged 8, makes friends with a gerenuk (giraffe-gazelle). Their name is derived from the Somali word garanuug (giraffe-necked). September 1954.

Gerbils Gerry and Joan's new home, a battered old suede boot that belonging to their keeper. October 1972.

Ally the polar bear chilling out on his terrace in April 1971. Polar bears had been a feature of the zoo since the 1850s, though they did not have appropriate accommodation until superintendent Gerald Iles was able to modernise it in the late 1930s. The next transformation came in 1960 when the whole area was remodelled as the Bear Terrace. The animals had more space to move around in, a more interesting terrain comprising rock formations, pools and a moat.

(Top right and right). This young polar bear was rejected by its mother at birth. The wife of one of Belle Vue's executives took the cub home and reared it for four months. Here the young bear is being reintroduced to the pool.

The latest arrivals at the Aquarium in August 1948. A new Aquarium and Reptile House was completed in 1964. It was sympathetically landscaped and attention to habitat detail was an intrinsic part of how the animals were displayed. In the main hall was a tropical forest section with a waterfall and large pool. Small birds flew around inside the glass structure. As visitors stepped over the bridge, they could view the alligators and crocodiles.

The Reptile House complete with pool, foliage, crocodiles and alligators. In 1965 a pair of American alligators mated. However, the eggs were infertile. This MEN photograph shows the female alligator guarding her nest.

By August 1968, school teacher Annette Timewell was concerned that her male tortoises James and Fez were failing to attract mates. She brought them along to the zoo where they were introduced to several females, but despite early signs that something positive might happen, both failed to mate. Not to be outdone Annette said: "Now I may have to try them with a couple of females from a pet shop."

George Wilburn 'Captain George' the sealion trainer holds a photograph of himself and his beloved sealions on the day he retired in October 1975. Sealions were reintroduced in 1947 and for several years appeared at the Christmas Circus.

Winston Taylor was curator of the Aquarium and Reptile House for more than 40 years. During his time, he witnessed many new arrivals – some by less conventional routes such as in boxes of fruit and vegetables at Smithfield Market.

It was during 1930 that Matt Kelly began his career as a zoo keeper, when he was hired by Dublin Zoo. The zoo was no stranger to the Kelly family, his older brother Thomas, their father and their grandfather, were either working or had worked there. By 1946, brother Thomas was Head Keeper at Dublin, and Matt applied for and got the position of Head Keeper at Belle Vue, a post vacant since the retirement of James Craythorne in 1944.

Like Gerald Iles, Matt was passionate about animals and keen to attract the maximum publicity for the zoo. The press would ring up every day asking if there were any stories and Matt would usually find something to interest them.

On one occasion, Matt himself was the centre of attention. He lost his grip on an adder he was holding only for the brute to sink its fangs into one of his fingers. He applied a tourniquet, told Gerald Iles what had happened and then headed off to hospital. Matt's wife was due to give birth any moment and has he did not want her upset, he made Iles promise not to tell her what had happened. At the time, the only stock of serum was held by London Zoo, so the police were asked to help. It took twelve hours for the serum to reach Manchester, by which time Matt was paralysed down one side and his vision impaired. Once the serum was administered Matt regained the use of his body but, against medical advice, discharged himself and headed for home. It was none too soon as his daughter was born soon after.

Matt loved to involve the wider community in the zoo. The images on this page show him with a group of visually impaired visitors. He would take them round, encouraging them touch some of the animals as well as ride on one of the elephants. (Both courtesy Collection Tommy Kelly).

Asian elephants Ellie May (left) and Ram Moti take delivery of new tyres courtesy the India Tyre Company. (Courtesy Collection Tommy Kelly).

Matt gives Nicholas the hippo a little TLC on his tusks. (Courtesy Collection Tommy Kelly).

Matt would often be asked to give talks at schools, to the Boy Scouts, Girl Guides, to working men's clubs and so on. He would take along a parrot, or a macaw, or a snake, or sometimes Azi the chimpanzee. He would also tip off the local press. We think this posed shot was taken in a working men's club. According to Tommy Kelly, it was unlikely Azi actually had any beer and that, in any case, the chimp had no chance of parting an Irishman from his beer. (Courtesy Collection Tommy Kelly).

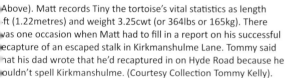

(Above). Matt records Tiny the tortoise's vital statistics as length
ft (1.22metres) and weight 3.25cwt (or 364lbs or 165kg). There
was one occasion when Matt had to fill in a report on his successful
recapture of an escaped stalk in Kirkmanshulme Lane. Tommy said
that his dad wrote that he'd recaptured in on Hyde Road because he
couldn't spell Kirkmanshulme. (Courtesy Collection Tommy Kelly).

Top right). Matt looks on as comedian Eric Morecambe takes the
scissors to the tape to officially open Belle Vue's new Great Ape
House. Eric then took the scissors to his partner Ernie Wise's tie.
Courtesy Collection Tommy Kelly).

Right).Not quite sure what Matt is up to with singing star Eartha
Kitt's leg. Eartha officially opened the Tropical River House on 25
March 1970. According to Tommy Kelly, after going around the
building, including entering the pygmy hippo pen, Eartha said to
Matt "Mi boots 'll be all smellie". We think Matt is tackling Eartha's
problem with an air freshener.

Zoological Superintendent Gerald Iles' career in broadcasting started on radio during the Second World War and continued into the television age. He is pictured here taking part in a Children's Hour broadcast at the BBC's Manchester Studios in the days when things went out live on air.

Having studied zoology at university, Iles joined Belle Vue as Zoological Superintendent in 1933 and from the very beginning sought to keep the zoo in the public eye. He was a great publicist, getting items about the zoo into the newspapers or on Pathe News whenever the opportunity arose. In 1955 the Chicago Zoo wanted to present Belle Vue with a polar bear named Aurora. However, Aurora's entry into the UK was blocked by the Board of Trade. Iles was not going to let a government department get in the way and contacted his friends in the press. They rallied to Belle Vue's aid, accusing the Board of Trade of an affront to the American people. It was too much for the BOT. They caved in and Aurora came to Belle Vue.

Gerald Iles was passionate about animals and wanted the zoo to be recognised as one of the leading centres for the care and study of animals. As vets had little or no knowledge of exotic species, Iles himself often carried out surgical procedures on the animals. When Iles left in 1957 to go and work in Montreal, Belle Vue lost one of the country's most experienced and highly regarded superintendents.

Gerald Iles died in Montreal in July 2004.

However, following Iles' departure, Belle Vue played an important part in the development of veterinary procedures for exotic animals. One day in 1957, the zoo called out the local veterinary practice to deal with a chimp that had lost a finger during a squabble over food. The vet who turned up was a recently qualified guy by the name of David Taylor. Taylor realised he did not know how to handle or anaesthetise the animal – or for that matter any other exotic species. Taylor was determined to change things, developing the veterinary skills and knowledge base now used at zoos throughout the world. In 1976 he founded the International Zoo Veterinary Group.

All the Fun of the Fair

Although there was a limited selection of funfair rides during the Jennison era, things changed dramatically when ownership of the gardens transferred to Belle Vue (Manchester) Ltd.

Under the guidance of managing director John Henry Iles, 1925 brought with it the introduction of new rides including the Caterpillar, Jack & Jill, the Dodgems, the Flying Sea Planes (a 1920s example of which can still be seen in Barcelona) and the Ghost Train. The Scenic Railway was also built in time for the 1925 season on the site of the Figure 8 Toboggan but did not become fully operational until 1927.

The image at top left shows the Lighthouse Slip, erected in 1906 next to the small lake. At the time, there were numerous names for this type of ride. The earliest known recorded use of helter-skelter was at Hull Fair in 1905. Other names included: alpine glide, Canadian glide and glacier slip. The building on the left of the image is the power house. It contained two 250hp steam engines to drive the site's electric generators. Built in 1897, it remained in use until the late 1920s when power was taken from the mains. The building was then converted into the Fish Restaurant. The small lake was excavated during 1853 to provide a home for birds that could no longer be kept on the Firework Lake. It was filled in during the mid-1920s.

Another ride from the Edwardian era was the Figure 8 Toboggan. James Jennison had observed one of these rides in action during a trip to White City, Stretford, and decided it was just what Belle Vue needed. It was erected in 1908 and located between a maze and the Paddock. It was replaced by the Scenic Railway.

August Bank Holiday 1949. There is not much evidence of ice cream or candyfloss as rationing was still in force. Food rationing was gradually eased from July 1948 and sweets came off ration the following year. But demand was such that they were put back on again and would remain so until 5 February 1953. Even then, the UK was importing sugar at just 53per cent of what it had been pre-war. After 14 years, food rationing finally came to an end on 4 July 1954, when restrictions on the sale of meat and bacon were lifted.

(Opposite page top). In May 1946, visitors were happy to queue for nearly an hour to experience all the thrills of the Bobs. The ride was known as the Bobs because it cost one shilling per person per go – an expensive ride even then as many travelling fair rides were priced at 3d (1p), 4d (2p) or 6d (2.5p). One shilling in decimal currency is 5p, however when taking inflation into account, the 2018 equivalent of that 5p is around £2.05p. Gerald Iles bought the Bobs second hand from a Mr Church from Buffalo, New York state, USA, for £20,000. Church advised Iles to run the Bobs intensively for a few years then scrap it. But the Bobs proved too popular – its ten-car trains hurtling along at speeds up to 61mph. Reaching a maximum height of 80ft and with down gradients of 45degrees, the Bobs was for many years the world's fastest gravity ride. In 2018, the world's fastest gravity ride was Kingda Ka at the Six Flags Great Adventure Park, New Jersey, USA. It accelerated from 0-128mph in 3.5 seconds. On The Big One (built 1994) at Blackpool Pleasure Beach, passengers experience a G-force of 3.5 as their cars plunge at 74mph.

(Opposite page bottom).The Bobs serves as a dramatic backdrop to another famous ride, the Caterpillar. The Caterpillar ran on a wave-like track. A canopy dropped over the car plunging its occupants into darkness. As the car moved round the track it got faster and faster. From the outside the car looked like a moving caterpillar.

All the thrills of the Bobs.

On the right are the Go-Karts and in the background is the Scenic Railway dating from 1926.

Daily Mirror Day at Belle Vue, June 1962. A candyfloss break, then over to the Helter-Skelter.

(Top left). A familiar sight at a merry-go-round. (Courtesy Jan Hollins).

Sunday best for a day out at Belle Vue in the 1950s. In the background is one of the funfair's merry-go-rounds. Beyond that is the back of the Scenic Railway. (Courtesy Jan Hollins).

The smaller boating lake was popular with kids of all ages. During the Salford floods of 1946, the lake's rowing boats were pressed into service ferrying people to safety. (Courtesy Jan Hollins).

(Left). The Water Chute nears completion. This is the view passengers would see as their car descended into the water. When the funfair closed, the ride was dismantled and moved to Blackpool Pleasure Beach where it was operated under the name Vikingar.

(Below). The first car to take passengers on Belle Vue's new ride for 1957 – The Water Chute – ploughs into the wet stuff. The passengers were Sir Leslie Joseph (managing director Belle Vue); speedway star Dick Fisher and his wife Jean; Belle Vue general manager J W Betts; retired speedway rider Ken Sharples and Belle Vue's publicity manager Johnny Hoskins, who lost his hat when the car splashed into the water. The Water Chute was built on the site once occupied by the 1936 Centenary floral clock and a large gibbon cage.

The miniature railway opened for business on 30 May 1928 and operated for 53 years. During that time, it underwent several incarnations. A return loop was added for the 1936 Centenary celebrations, though the biggest change came in 1964 when the track was laid to allow trains to run on a continuous circuit around the Small Lake. Part of the route was through the zoo, taking in Wolf Wood, the Lion and Tiger Enclosures and the Marsupial Enclosures. The railway was rebranded as the Santa Fe and the locomotives were fitted with American balloon smoke stacks and cowcatchers. In 1971 it reverted back to the Belle Vue Railway and closed in 1977.

Circus Circus

The annual Christmas Circus was an institution in the North West for nearly six decades, bringing thrills, spills, excitement and wonders to the countless people who sat enthralled under its big top. The circus was amongst the finest in Europe and no expense was spared on bringing the best acts to Belle Vue.

The first circus was held in 1922 but does not appear to have been a success. The idea was put on hold until 1929, when Gerald Iles and his father William collaborated with Tom Bickerstaff of the Blackpool Tower Company to bring the Blackpool circus acts and equipment to Belle Vue for Christmas. An early transfer was George Lockhart – a man who went on to achieve legendary status in the world of circus as the "Prince of Ringmasters."

Lockhart reigned at Belle Vue for an unbelievable 43 years. His personality left an indelible mark over the entire operation – he was as much a part of the Circus as was the Kings Hall where it was staged. The 1967/68 season was George's 39th consecutive year in charge and the circus was renamed the "George Lockhart Celebration Circus." in his honour.

Another name linked with the history of the circus is Fred Bonelli. As a young man, Fred had played trumpet with Barnum & Bailey's Band. He went on to become a great bandleader, arranger and composer. He conducted the circus band for more than 30 years.

During the Second World War, Lockhart was put in sole charge of the circus. There was a severe lack of acts and staff, as well as limits imposed by the Defence Regulations as to when performances could take place.

One act that first appeared at Belle Vue during the war years was Pepino's Miniature Circus. It was a sort of music hall meets the big top, Pepino's circus consisting of a pony, a monkey and a few dogs performing variety of tricks including one of the dogs riding on the pony's back. After the war, Pepino remained at Belle Vue and every summer would set up shop in a building that had originally housed Jennison's Steam Horses. Pepino's circus survived into the 1960s.

Over the years, hundreds of internationally acclaimed acts performed at the Kings Hall. Many visitors thought that the animals they saw performing had simply been borrowed from Belle Vue Zoo. This was not the case though there were exceptions. Since 1947, the zoo's sea lions had been performing in a display devised by their keeper Captain Harry Smith and his wife Evelyn. They were both Germans and Schmidt was their real name. The sea lions went through a routine that included playing trumpets and juggling a giant-sized ball. So, from 1948 to 1953, the sea lions along with Captain Harry and Evelyn appeared in the Christmas shows. The other exception was in 1952/53 when Gerald Iles staged a 'Noah's Ark' feature.

The job of taking over as Ringmaster after the departure of George Lockhart was a difficult task. But Norman Barrett, a man with a long history in the circus, took the job. As well as presiding over the show, Barrett was well known for his own act with performing budgerigars. During his career, he worked with all the world's great circuses, including 25 years with the Blackpool Tower Circus. In 1990 he was the subject of a BBC TV This is Your Life show, and in 2010 he was awarded the MBE. He presided over the last circus to be held within the Kings Hall.

Gilbert Honche and his tigers at Belle Vue, January 1947. Honche, aged 29, performed with up to six fully grown Royal Bengal tigers – each of them weighing in at around 190kg.

(Above). Charly Bohm goes through his routine during rehearsals for the 24th International Circus. A handy guy to have around should you need to move any furniture.

(Top left). The Three Torellis during rehearsals for the 21st International Circus (1949-50). Their Adagio Continental act often involved them dressing Parisian underworld style – hooped T shirts, baggy trousers and berets for the guys; slit skirt, blouse, beret for the girl. Their brilliantly executed routine involved pirouettes and much throwing and catching of the girl – all to appropriate music.

One of Rudi Lenz's chimpanzees, Toby, hams it up for the press. Toby featured on the cover of the souvenir programme for the 31st International Circus.

The 41st International circus featured Harry Belli and his horse-riding tiger: to say nothing of the dog! Harry ran a small circus in the Netherlands. The tiger was called Byla, the horse Bulle and the dog Jimmy.

If Harry's act was unusual, Robert Bros' Berkshire pigs was unique. Bought as piglets for £10 each, these highly intelligent animals were the only performing pig act in the UK. At the time the pigs were valued at £400 each – approximately £6,260 in 2018.

41st International Circus. Featured here are the Schlingloff Troupe. Other acts appearing included: Willi Mullens Caucasian Cavalry and Ponies; Strong Man Samson with Delilah; The Glamorous Inaros Sisters; Armand Elleano live wire act; Les Chabres with oodles of Poodles; as well as clowns Alby, Jacko, Noe-Noe and Billy.

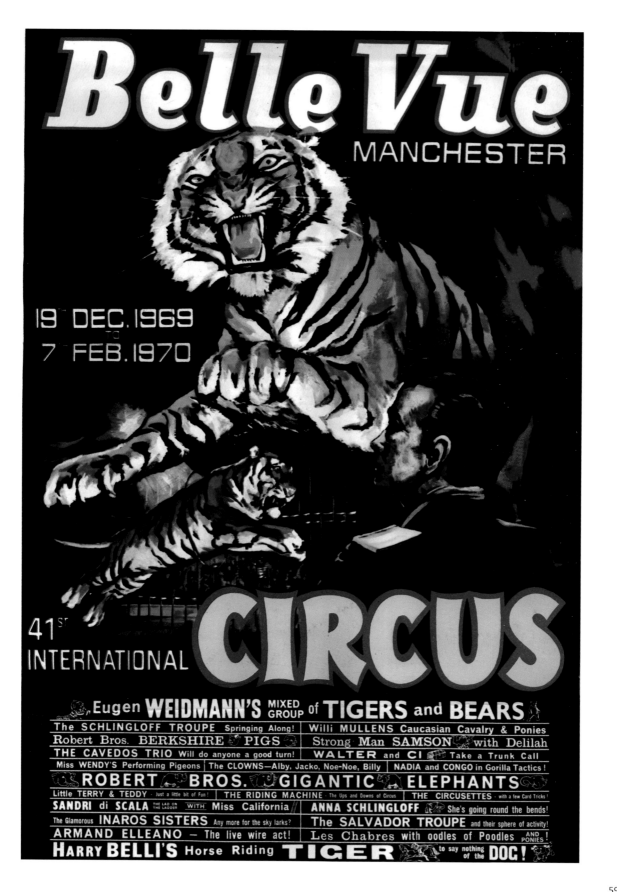

41st International Circus. The Salvador Troupe go through their routine.

41st International Circus. Miss Wendy performs her balancing act. Her partner during this element was a pigeon perched on the end of sword.

(Below left). Belle Vue's Golden Jubilee Circus ran from 22 December 1978 to 3 February 1979. Here, Jacko the Clown walks around the edge of the circus ring, squirting water from his hat, giving the audience a ducking and a laugh.

(Below). It was great being circus kids. Back in 1969, Carol (aged 4) and Grace (aged 2), were the daughters of clown Carlos McManus. Grace looks on as Carol shows off her balancing skills. Carlos was at Belle Vue to take part in the 41st International Circus.

Former bareback rider Norman Barrett was one of the few ringmasters capable of taking over from the irrepressible George Lockhart.

The ring. The restricted height of the Kings Hall made it difficult for high wire and flying trapeze acts to perform here.

Santa Claus returns to Belle Vue to let people know that the traditional Christmas Circus for 1981-82 will go ahead. In the background, the Kings Hall is being demolished. This was the last circus held under an agreement between Trust House Forte and the site's new owners, the Espley Tyas Development Group. It turned out not to be the final curtain.

The following Christmas, Robert Brothers Circus used the Speedway Stadium as a site. Robert Fosset, better known as Jacko the Clown, outside the Robert Brothers big top at the Speedway Stadium. Jacko began his circus career in a trapeze act alongside his three sisters. His career as a clown included a thirty-year partnership with Little Billy Merchant.

Robert Brothers returned for Christmas 1983-84 though this time the circus was housed in the Exhibiton Hall. Jacko Fossett and Maureen the elephant are pictured at Belle Vue promoting the show in September 1983. The 1984-85 and 1985-86 shows were given by Circus Hoffman.

Direct from the Cirque d'Hiver, Paris, the Biagre Family's juggling act comprised Esmerelda Briatton and her two 'spinning' brothers. Their act opened with the three of them heading a large beach ball – their skills on a par with any Premier League footballer you care to name, before going on to the complicated stuff pictured here. As a child, Esmerelda had contracted polio though it did not hinder her performance.

One of the Robert Brothers Circus riders ready for the evening performance in the Exhibition Hall. The circus ran from Friday, 23 December 1983 to Sunday, 22 January 1984. Tickets prices were: Ringside, £4 for adults and £3 for children; centre tiers, £3 and £2; side tiers, £2 and £1.50.

Thorson Kohrmann and his Farmyard Friends. The goats do their stuff, but the pig looks a little bored.

Brenda Hani goes through her elephant act.

(Above). Oooo! Clown's hat on fire. Still it's Jacko to the rescue and someone is going to get wet. Over the years, Belle Vue had its fair share of great clowns. From Tambo and Tambo, Ross and Willie, Ross Adam, Johnco, and of course Jacko Fosset. Jacko caused mayhem and humour in a partnership with Little Billy Merchant.

(Above right). The object of the exercise in an impalement act is to get the axe or knife as close to the assistant's body as possible without causing injury. Among the famous impalement acts since the Second World War are The Brumbachs/Los Alamos and the Two Tornados. Fritz Brumbach started his act with his wife, Helga, as the target. They were later joined by their daughter, Sylvia, who acted as a second target, and son Patrick became a thrower. Fritz Brumbach holds the world record for rapid throwing around his target.

The Two Tornados were husband and wife Rolf and Irene Stey. Part of their act included Rolf throwing knives blindfolded. They were one of only two acts that staged the combined 'Wheel of Death' and tightrope stunt. It involved Irene being strapped to the target board which was then spun round. Rolf would then throw knives or axes whilst balancing on a tightrope.

(Right). The Bogino Brothers performing to an admiring crowd.

Music

The park's first ballroom was situated above the Longsight entrance. It opened in 1851 and stood for just over a hundred years before being demolished as unsafe for further use. The next musical innovation occurred a couple of years later when Belle Vue staged its first brass band competition. When John Jennison visited the Great Exhibition during 1851, he observed just how popular music competitions were and brought the idea back with him. At the time, Belle Vue already had its own brass band but Jennison thought it under-used and a competition or two would cast it into the limelight. A trial contest was organised in 1852. Declared a success both in musical and financial terms, Jennison organised a proper event for the following year. It too proved a huge success and annual competitions were held for the next 33 years. From 1886, a second brass band competition was held and in 1900 a series of military band contests took place. At the time, all regiments in the British Army had bands, as well as Royal Marines Divisional Bands at naval bases.

During the 1930s, efforts were made to bring the park up-to-date. The Kings Hall was remodelled, turning from a basic hall into an all-seated arena. It allowed the venue to host a variety of performances including classical, popular music, jazz and big bands. It could also host rallies, meetings, and the circus.

One of the first events staged at the Kings Hall after the Second World War, was on 8 June 1945, featuring Albert Sandler and Richard Tauber. Sandler was a leading light in the world of light classical music and had been a popular orchestra leader during the 1930s. Richard Tauber was a tenor. An Austrian, Tauber had been robbed of his citizenship by the Nazis. He settled in Switzerland until arrangements could be made to bring him to the UK in 1940. He had spent much of the war making records and working in radio.

Before the decade was out, Belle Vue had hosted the Berlin Philharmonic, the Philadelphia Philharmonic, and Yehudi Menuhin and the Liverpool Philharmonic orchestras. During 1949, Beniamio Gigli, the Italian Opera singer considered to have been one of the finest tenors of his generation, sang at sell-out concerts on 10 March and again on 25 October.

On 8 May 1951, Belle Vue audiences were treated to the sounds of the Festival of Britain, Royal Philharmonic Orchestra and the following year the Vienna Philharmonic. As well as classical music, Belle Vue accommodated jazz and big band. Count Basie, Louis Armstrong and the Lionel Hampton Orchestra all appeared.

However, it was in November 1956 that Belle Vue experience the somewhat new phenomena of teenage girls screaming at their idol, when the Nabob of Sob, the Prince of Wails, Johnnie Ray, performed. The following year, the place rocked when Manchester rock 'n' rollers competed for tickets to see Bill Haley and the Comets.

From May 1963, the New Elizabethan became the venue for a Sunday night Top Ten Club. Billed locally as "the largest teenage dance club in the country", it ran until 1970. Unfortunately, for much of the time, it was compared by the wretched Jimmy Saville.

Throughout the sixties and seventies, Belle Vue's popularity as a venue for live music continued. The Rolling Stones, The Who, Jimi Hendrix, Led Zeppelin, T.Rex, Johnny Cash, The Bay City Rollers, David Cassidy and Bob Marley and the Wailers, were just a few the acts that played to capacity crowds.

Built over a six-week period in 1910 for the staging of exhibitions, demonstrations and for what the Edwardians referred to as 'social gatherings,' the venue was named after the two kings whose reigns the construction fell within - Edward V11 and George V.

The Ballroom. The original ballroom was above the Longsight entrance to the park and could accommodate up to 500 people but was demolished in the 1950s as unfit for further use.

Rochdale's very own Gracie Fields performing on stage in 1938 when she was at the peak of her popularity. As well as performing shows in London, Gracie toured the provinces, appearing at Belle Vue in April 1938. Already a Freeman of the Borough of Rochdale, Gracie was awarded a CBE (for services to entertainment) in February 1938 and the following May was made an Officer of the Venerable Order of St John of Jerusalem (for charity work). During 1939 she became seriously ill with cervical cancer, receiving around 250,000 get well messages and cards from her fans. She was still recovering at her villa on Capri when World War II broke out. She immediately enlisted for ENSA.

During the 1930s, an appearance at Belle Vue by Gracie Fields was guaranteed to pull in the

crowds. On 1 May 1936, Gracie opened the new aquarium. Unfortunately, the zoo was still awaiting delivery of many of the fish due to be housed there, so Gerald Iles was forced to delay Gracie whilst staff spread around what fish they had so there were no empty tanks. In 1959, Gracie inaugurated a new attraction, the Wall of Fame, Belle Vue's answer to Grauman's Chinese Theatre, Hollywood, where stars left impressions of their hands and feet in concrete blocks.

Boys of Chetham's Hospital School rehearing for a British Legion Remembrance Service that was held at Belle Vue.

Peruvian-American soprano Yma Sumac singing to a capacity audience at the Kings Hall, in June 1952 during her first tour of Europe and Africa. Sumac had risen to international stardom thanks to her tremendous vocal range – said to be over five octaves. She recorded several albums, starred on Broadway and appeared in movies.

(Above). The Lionel Hampton Orchestra kicked off its first UK tour at the Empress Hall, London, on 21 October 1956, and played 27 venues including the Kings Hall on 4th November. Hampton was famed for mainstream jazz, swing and big band. However, this tour was surrounded by controversy because he included rock 'n' roll numbers. It is said that John Dankworth walked out of a concert in disgust and the *Melody Maker* magazine printed letters of complaint from disgruntled fans.

(Left). Possibly some of the earliest instances of teenage girls screaming at their idol occurred at Johnnie Ray concerts. Ray had several nicknames: The Nabob of Sob and The Prince of Wails being just two of them. Ray appeared at Belle Vue in November 1956, having recently climbed to the top of the UK singles chart with *Just Walkin' In the Rain*. The record gave Ray his longest run in the UK singles charts – 19 weeks. In 1954, Ray had a UK number one single with *Such A Night* and his third and final UK number one would come during 1957 with *Yes Tonight Josephine*. His last single to chart in the UK was during December 1959, when *I'll Never Fall in Love Again* made it to number 26 during a six-week run. Ray certainly knew how to work the room thanks to his uncanny ability to cry at will.

Manchester rock 'n' roll fans compete for tickets in the *Daily Mirror's* Bill Haley Contest held at Belle Vue on 7 February 1957. Haley's first tour of the UK was largely sponsored by the *Daily Mirror*.

Promoted by Harold Davidson, who had also promoted Lionel Hampton, Louis Armstrong and his All-Stars opened the UK part of their 1959 European Tour on 28 February, with a two-night date at the Gaumont State, Kilburn, and performed at the Kings Hall on 9 March. It was a killer of a tour, the band performing two shows a day at most venues.

The All-Stars comprised some of the most talented jazz musicians of the day including: Danny Barcelona on drums, Peanuts Hucko on clarinet, Billy Kyle on piano, Jack Lesberg on double bass, and Trummy Young on trombone.

One of the best-known musicians ever to have lived, "Satchmo" was instantly recognisable – gravelly voice, trumpet and handkerchief. Born in 1901, Armstrong learnt to play the trumpet whilst in a children's home, where he was sent for firing a gun in the air. Throughout the 30s and 40s, "Satchmo" carved out a reputation as a supremely talented musician, playing all over the United States and Europe. Armstrong kept up an exhausting touring regime until his death.

Scheduled for May-June 1958, the 27-date UK tour by Jerry Lee Lewis was to have been the biggest ever undertaken by an American rock 'n' roller. It ended in chaos when it was found that Lewis's new wife Myra was only 13 years old, though the marriage was perfectly legal under US law. There were no such problems with his 12-date, Jerry Lee Lewis Show, tour of March-April 1964. The show, which played at the Kings Hall on 29 March, also featured Gene Vincent, The Paramounts, The Animals, the Nashville Teens, the Flintstones and Tony Adams and the Viceroys. The show was compered by Peter Kaye. Seat prices were: 10/6 (52.5p), 8/6 (42.5p) and 6/6 (32.5p).

Rolling Stones drummer Charlie Watts in action at the New Elizabethan Ballroom on 9 August 1964. The Stones were part way through their third UK tour of the year, though the previous day they had nipped over to the Netherlands to play a gig in Scheveningen. The Stones were back in Manchester on 15 September, playing two shows at the Odeon.

The Rolling Stones 1973 European Tour comprised a total 42 shows spread across 22 cities. Mick Jagger is pictured here strutting his stuff in the Kings Hall where the band played on 11th and 12th September. The gig at the Deutschlandhalle, West Berlin, turned out to be Mick Taylor's last live performance with the Stones.

(Opposite page). Fans screamed and some fainted when David Cassidy played at Belle Vue, the first UK venue on his 1973 European tour. There were two shows each evening; 5.30pm for the teenyboppers, 8.00pm for older fans.

(Bottom). The Jackson Five photographed before their appearance at the Kings Hall on 10 November 1972. Left to right are: Jackie, Tito, Marlon, Michael and Jermaine. Jumping in the air is Randy Jackson – the youngest brother. Randy made his first official appearance with his brothers at a special Christmas charity concert in 1971. He did not join the family band until 1975 when he replaced Jermaine.

The Who's legendary drummer Keith Moon. The nights of 1 and 2 November 1973, saw the group play the Kings Hall for the first time. Both nights were sell-outs. However, Mooney had played the venue earlier in the year when it was used for location filming for the movie Stardust, starring David Essex. He appeared in the film as the drummer of The Stray Cats. The Who returned to Belle Vue for two nights in October 1976. Again, both nights were sell-outs.

(Opposite page). The Bay City Rollers played to a sell-out crowd on 12 September 1976. At top left, we have at back, left to right: Eric Faulkner, Les McKeown, Stuart Wood. Front: Derek Longmuir and Ian Mitchell. At top right, Les McKeown on stage at the Kings Hall. At bottom, screaming Bay City Rollers' fans are held back by security men as they attempt to reach the stage.

Slade were at the height of their fame when they played Belle Vue. In early 1973, their single *Cum on Feel the Noize* was the first since the Beatles' Get Back in 1969 to go straight to number one in the UK charts on its release.

Following the break-up of the Faces, Rod Stewart moved to Los Angeles, where he formed the Rod Stewart Group with Carmine Appice, Jim Cregan, Billy Peek, Phil Chen, Gary Grainger and John Jarvis. He is pictured here with ex-Cockney Rebel Jim Cregan at Belle Vue in November 1976. Cregan and Stewart formed a writing partnership that would see them credited with 30 recorded songs. Rod Stewart returned to Belle Vue for a gig on 3 December 1978.

Punk rockers Souxsie and the Banshees appeared along with the Clash at the Elizabethan Ballroom on 15 November 1977. The band returned in December for a two-date gig, playing solo on the 17th and joined the following night by the Buzzcocks (who had supported the Sex Pistols on their Anarchy tour) and the Penetration, who also had a female lead vocalist (Pauline Murray). Souxsie's next appearance in Manchester was at the university on 4 November 1978.

Phil Lynott of Thin Lizzy. Though formed in Dublin, Lynott's mother owned a hotel in Manchester which is the subject of their album track, Clifton Grange Hotel. In May 1976, they reached number six in the singles charts with *The Boys Are Back in Town*, about the group's visits to Manchester. They played at Belle Vue in June 1978.

The Clash appeared at the Elizabethan Ballroom during their 32-date *Get Out of Control Tour*. Left to right: drummer Nicky 'Topper' Headon, lead vocalist/rhythm guitarist Joe Strummer, bassist Paul Simonon and vocalist/lead guitarist Mick Jones. (Below). Debris litters the foyer after fans got a little out of control.

Participants in the Annual Brass Band Contest for 1958. It is not known who came up with the idea to hold an annual brass band contest, though it is thought that Belle Vue's founder John Jennison was encouraged to do so by James Melling, conductor of the City Royal Brass Band. When John Henry Iles took over at Belle Vue in 1929, he already had a strong connection with brass band music competitions, so it was natural, therefore, that he would bring them with him. Brass Band competitions played an important role in the continuing popularity of Belle Vue. Competition audiences would often fill the Kings Hall to capacity.

Sport

As early as 1847, sport began to play a part in Belle Vue's history when a racecourse was added to the early site. This particular venture proved unsuccessful, but it laid the foundation for many more sporting facilities and events that enthralled the public for more than a century.

It was in 1887 that sport found a permanent base in Belle Vue when the Jennison family built an athletics ground near Hunters Lane. The facilities were good enough in 1920 for Manchester City FC to enter into negotiations over leasing the stadium after fired destroyed the main stand at their Hyde Road ground. The discussions proved unproductive, however, and City eventually moved to a newly-built ground at Maine Road in 1923.

When the new company gained control in 1925, a wave of new investment in sporting facilities followed. The company was controlled by Sir William Gentle, Captain J P Hodge and John Henry Iles. Sir William was one of the founding members of the International Greyhound Racing Association and he and Captain Hodge built the first greyhound stadium in the UK on land leased from Belle Vue. Eventually, they would both leave Belle Vue (Manchester) Ltd to concentrate on this new sport.

Control of the company then passed to Iles and it was he who brought speedway – or dirt track as it was then known - to the park. The first meeting, organised by International Speedway, was held on 28 July 1928 in the Greyhound Stadium. Soon, meetings were being organised by Eric Oliver Spence (E O Spence) and his North Manchester Motor Club. Spence was already heavily involved with speedway and when Iles acquired the controlling interest in the North Manchester Motor Club, he appointed E O Spence as speedway manager.

Iles and Spence believed that the club would be better served if it had its own purpose-built stadium on the Belle Vue site. Work rapidly went ahead, the first meeting being held on 23 March 1929. The early speedway meetings were individual events of varying types, though eventually team races became popular with the public.

In 1933 Belle Vue won both the National League Champions and National Trophy Winners cups. E O Spence strived constantly to bring the best riders to Belle Vue and a consequence of this was changing the team's name in 1934 to the Belle Vue Aces. During the Second World War, the Aces managed to keep going thanks to a combination of guest riders on leave from the armed forces and talented youngsters, managing to stage an incredible 170 senior meetings between 1939 and 1945.

In 1941, E O Spence retired as speedway manager to become managing director of the Belle Vue Company. His place was taken by Alice Hart, who held the post until 1952. Johnnie Hoskins then took over and it was he who was responsible for bringing stock car racing to the park.

1928 was also the year the Belle Vue Company formed Manchester Central FC as Iles was convinced East Manchester ought to have its own professional League Football side. The legendary Manchester City, Manchester United and Wales international Billy Meredith was signed on as coach. However, Central's bid for League status was foiled when City and United objected.

During 1930, the Kings Hall was given a facelift, turning it into a 5,000-seat venue, ideal for wrestling and boxing. The first wrestling contest held there was on 15 December 1930 and featured Bert Assirati and Atholl Oakley. Interestingly, the promotion of wrestling at Belle Vue was taken over by Miss Kathleen Look, the only female promoter in the country. She was married to E O Spence. By the late 1930s, the venue had become a magnet for wrestling fans. Later in the 1940s, husband and wife team Jessie and Dick Rodgers promoted the sport.

Ever the showman, Iles instigated a number of other sports that used the speedway stadium as their home with varying degrees of success. Rugby Union, baseball, American football, tennis, even chariot racing, were some of them.

Though Belle Vue's aspirations for a professional League football team had come to nothing, the rugby union team faired better.

roughton Rangers were founded in 1877 at roughton, Salford, and were one of the 21 sides hat in 1895 formed the Northern Rugby Football nion. In 1933 they left Salford and moved to elle Vue Stadium, becoming Belle Vue Rangers 1946. They reached the final of the 1946-47 ancashire Cup, losing 9-3 to Wigan. The following eason, they again reached the final and again ost to Wigan, though this time it was 10-3. The lub's fortunes began to wane, and they finished he 1954-55 season in 30th position, the Rangers olding shortly after.

hroughout the club's history it had its fair share f players who won international honours. mong them was Ray Price, capped six times for Vales whilst playing for Belle Vue Rangers; Elwyn iwyther, capped for Wales (RL)

as well as for Great Britain, and Doug Phillips who was also capped for Great Britain.

Of all the sports tried out at Belle Vue, only speedway, stock car and greyhound racing stood the test of time. But even then, the Aces had to move following the sale in 1987 of the Speedway Stadium to British Car Auctions. The final event at the Stadium was a stock car meeting on 14 November. The Aces found a new home. They moved to the Greyhound Stadium, ironically where they had started life in 1929.

ome of the most memorable names in the history of Belle Vue speedway lined up for this photograph in 1933. Left to right: Eric Langton, Max irosskreutz, Bronc Dixon, Bob Harrison, Frank Varey and Bill Kitchen. Eric Langton was ever present in the Belle Vue squads of the thirties and orties. Born in Leeds in 1907, Langton's career began before the advent of speedway as a talented road racer and trials rider. He took to the ew sport and with his brother Oliver, pioneered many innovations such as using lightweight machines and different riding techniques.

The Belle Vue squad pictured in 1936 after winning their fourth consecutive National League title. Left to right: Bill Kitchen, Max Grosskreutz, Oliver Langton, Stanley 'Acorn' Dobson, Tommy Price, Joe Abbott, Bob Harrison and Frank Varey. Dobson had been christened 'Acorn' after someone had pointed out that his head looked like one.

Speedway legend Jack Parker signing autographs. Parker began his speedway career in 1929 with Coventry. He joined the Aces in 1946 and soon established his reputation as one of the country's great riders of the 1940s. His team honours included National Trophy Winner in 1946, 1947 and 1949, and National League Cup Winner 1946. Individual honours were the British Riders' Championship in 1947, and runner-up in the 1949 World Championship.

Left to right: Wally Lloyd, Geoff Pymar and Lionel van Praag in action at Belle Vue in 1947. Lionel van Praag was an Australian and in 1936 he won the inaugural Speedway World Championship. During the 1930s he rode for the Wembley Lions but with the outbreak of war joined the Royal Australian Air Force, winning the George Medal for bravery. After the war, he rode one season for New Cross Rangers and eventually gave up speedway to concentrate on his flying career.

Jack Rowley of Manchester United presenting Aces rider Jack Parker (centre) with the 1947 British Riders' Championship trophy. On the left is runner-up Aub Lawson. This individual speedway competition was held for three years beginning in 1946 when it was won by Tommy Price of the Wembley Lions. The 1948 title was taken by Vic Duggan of the Harringay Racers. Parker held the match race champion's title throughout 1948 and 1949, losing it at the end of 1950 to none other Aub Lawson.

Former Belle Vue Aces star Bill Kitchen, wearing the red and white tabard of the Wembley Lions, takes on Wally Lloyd.

Belle Vue battle the Wimbledon Dons.

Dent Oliver (left) with Louis Lawson in 1948. Oliver began his career in speedway with the Belle Vue Aces in 1946, making such an impression that he was called up to the England side for the 1947-48 Ashes test series in Australia. Dent stayed at Belle Vue until retiring from the sport in 1950.

However, he did not put his feet up for long. In 1951 the Bradford Tudors persuaded him to get back in the saddle and ride for them. In 1952, Belle Vue signed him for the second time but Oliver stayed only one season before returning to the Tudors. He rode for the Bradford side until retiring again in 1954. Two years later, he came out of retirement to ride in nine meetings for the Tudors and promptly retired for the third time.

In 1963, Frank Varey talked Oliver into again coming out of retirement, this time to ride for the Sheffield Tigers in the Provincial League. Oliver stayed with the Tigers for two seasons before signing for Belle Vue for the third time. After a handful of rides, he retired from racing but remained on the staff, becoming team manager in 1967. Under Oliver, the Aces won the British League in 1970, 1971 and 1972. The following year, Oliver became seriously ill and died on 15 December 1973 aged just 55.

Louis Lawson also joined the Aces in 1946, remaining with them until retiring in 1953. During his career he was in the 1946, 1947 and 1949 National Trophy winning sides, and rode in the 1949 and 1951 World Finals as well as being the reserve rider for the 1953 event.

On the day after his sixteenth birthday, Peter Craven went along to the Stanley Stadium, Liverpool, were his brother Brian rode for the Liverpool Chads speedway team. Mounting his brother's bike, Peter set off. It all went swimmingly for a few laps and then he collided with a safety barrier. Despite suffering from concussion, his enthusiasm did not wane, and the Liverpool Chads gave him a second chance.

He made eight appearances for the Chads before signing for Belle Vue, making his debut on 17 May 1952 in the meeting against the Norwich Stars. Despite being called up for national service, he rode in 12 matches in 1953, scoring 70 points. The following year he was the side's top scorer and qualified for his first World Championship, which he won, beating the Swedish rider Ove Fundin by one point.

Success followed success, including being three-times winner of the Pride of the East title; twice winner of the Pride of the Midlands title; British Champion in 1962 and 1963, and a second World Championship also in 1963. On 20 September, just a few days after securing his World Championship, Craven was at the Old Meadowbank Stadium, Edinburgh, to take part in a challenge match. During his fourth outing, he swerved to avoid fallen race leader George Hunter and hit a fence. The unconscious Craven was rushed to hospital where he died on 24 September, aged just 29. In 1967 the Peter Craven Memorial Trophy Meeting was held for the first time. It was won by Ivan Mauger.

As well as riding in the Swedish leagues, Soren Sjosten competed for the Belle Vue Aces (1962-64 and 1967-75), Birmingham Brummies (1976), Wolverhampton Wolves (1977), and Bristol Bulldogs (1978).

During a career spanning two decades, he won numerous team honours including the 1974 World Pairs Championship with Anders Michanek, and the 1962, 1964 and 1970 World Team Cups. His individual honours were 1959 Swedish Junior Champion and the 1965 Nordic Champion.

He had a reputation for being a fast starter. His riding style of taking bends at speed, thereby making his rear wheel slide further out than usual, made him a firm favourite with Aces' fans.

He retired from the sport in 1979 following the death of his brother Christer at a speedway meeting in Brisbane, Australia.

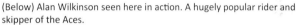

(Below) Alan Wilkinson seen here in action. A hugely popular rider and skipper of the Aces.

On 1 July 1978, Belle Vue were at home to Swindon, when at the first turn of the first race, Alan Wilkinson tangled with Swindon's Geoff Bouchard and smashed into the solid white boards between bends 1 and 2. The accident left Wilkinson confined to a wheelchair. Two years later, rider Mike Lohmann hit the same boards. Though he managed to return to speedway, he was never the same.

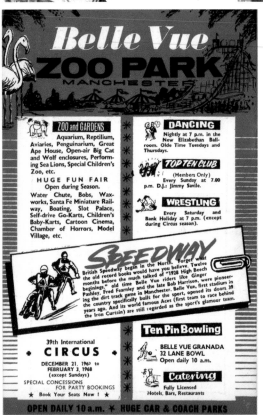

The Aces and Leicester teams go at it. Leicester skipper Ray Wilson (No.1) holds back teammate Alan Cowland (No.4) while officials grab Aces rider Alan Wilkinson.

(Opposite page top and bottom). Riders past and present at Belle Vue during the team's golden jubilee celebrations.

Ivan Mauger with the British League Speedway Rider's Championship trophy. Mauger arrived at Belle Vue in 1969 and the legendary Kiwi quickly established a reputation for showing single-minded determination when racing. He led the Aces to three Championships and a Knockout Cup. Having won two FIM Championship Gold Medals in succession, two American speedway fans, George Wenn and Ray Bokelman, promised to gold-plate his bike if he won a third. He did. They did. Mauger's triple gold bike, as it was known, was plated with 24 carat gold. The work took 18 months and cost $700,000 New Zealand Dollars.

Mauger had an incredible career. Six World Speedway Championships, three World Longtrack Championships, four World Team Cup Championships, four European Championships, two British-Nordic Championships, four British Championships, and one Intercontinental Championship.

In August 2016, his triple gold bike was bought by Canterbury Museum, New Zealand, for $1.7million NZD.

(Opposite page bottom). The senior squad in March 1983. Left to right: Andy Smith, Keny McKinna, Peter Ravn, Martin Scarisbrick, Larry Moss, skipper Chris Morton on the bike, Louis Carr, Peter Carr, Peter Collins and David Bargh.

Though signed by the Aces, Daveyhulme-born Chris Morton made his speedway debut whilst on loan to the Ellesmere Port Gunners on 15 May 1973. The following month, he made his Aces debut in an away meeting at Cradley Heath where he scored six individual points.

He rode for the Aces until his retirement in 1990 and amassed numerous individual and team honours. Some of his individual honours are: the 1974 British under-21 Champion; 1980 Intercontinental Champion; 1983 and 1987 Northern Riders Champion and 1984 British Riders League Champion. His team honours include: 1975, 1976, 1977 and 1978 Northern Trophy; 1973 and 1975 British League Knockout Cup and with Peter Collins won the 1984 World Pairs Championship.

He returned to the Aces in 2005 as commercial manager and was later a part of the consortium that bought the club. After a spell as team manager, he was appointed operations director.

Below). The Aces take on the Colts on the opening night of the 1984 season. The Aces finished the season in second place on 49points. The Ipswich Witches, on 51points, were champions, and the Cradley Heath Heathens were third with 44points.

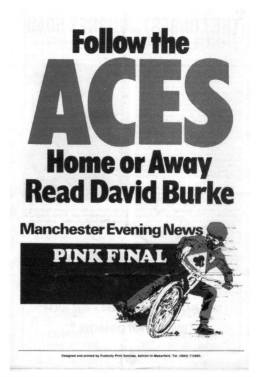

The Aces with their British League trophies. At left is Stuart Bamforth, who, as a driver, won the 1976 world stock car championships. Under Bamforth, the Aces won both the 1983 League Cup and Premiership. It was Bamforth who sold the stadium to British Car Auctions in 1987. To the right of Bamforth are: Peter Carr, Rod Hunter, Chris Morton (on bike), Larry Ross, Andy Smith, Peter Ravn (kneeling), Jimmy McMillan, Louis Carr, Peter Collins and team manager Ian Thomas. Thomas became hooked on speedway when he was just seven years old, and, though he never made it as a rider, became an influential promoter. He brought speedway to Workington and managed various teams including the Aces during 2005 and 2006. It was Thomas who introduced Premier League Pairs and Fours. He died in February 2011 following a long illness.

(Opposite page top). Manager Gordon Smith with Belle Vue's team for the new Junior League 1993. Left to right: Peter Scully, Mike Hampson and Jon Armstrong.

(Opposite page bottom). Aces speedway team, March 1993. Back row, left to right: Don Perrin, Jason Lyons, Frede Schott, Bobby Ott, Joe Screen, Mike Lushwaite, Carl Stonehewer, John Bose. Front left: Shawn Moran. Front right: Shawn Venables.

500cc racing cars at Belle Vue in August 1955. Midget dirt track racing started in the US in the 1930s and by 1935 had reached the UK. At Belle Vue it was promoted by E O Spence as Speedway Car Racing, spectator entry prices being 1/-, 2/- or 3/-, about the same as a night at the cinema. However, the outbreak of war led to a suspension of race meetings for the duration. When it resumed after the war, it never really regained its 1930s popularity.

Speedway manager Johnnie Hoskins was responsible for bringing stock car racing to Belle Vue, the first meeting taking place on 16 June 1954. As the sport grew in popularity, it became more organised. In August 1955, Hoskins organised a one-race World Championship which was won by Jerry Woltowicz.

GREYHOUND
Racing Association Ltd.
BELLE VUE, MANCHESTER

OPENING
MEETING

JULY 24TH, 1926
At 7-30 p.m.

SIX RACES
Prizes for Each Event—First £10 ; Second £5.

Judges :
Mr. O. A. CRITCHLEY, Major L. LYNE DIXSON, Mr. L. O. BROWN.
Timekeeper : Mr. E. WILKINSON.
Paddock Steward and Starter : Mr. W. SMITH.
Racing Secretary : Mr. MURRAY WILSON.

The name of any dog unable to compete in a race will be shown on the blackboard in each enclosure.

ALLIED NEWSPAPERS LTD., Printers, Withy Grove, Manchester.

FIRST RACE

¼ Mile.   7-30 p.m.
                                                              Colours.

1—Mr. W. R. Stewart ....r.d. MISTLEY (Jack-in-Office—Duck) .... Red 6/1
2—Lady Nash ....bd. & w.d. PARAMETER (Great Form—Littleworth Lament) Blue 10/1
3—Mr. Charles Munn, Jnr......r. or f.d. CRYPTOGRAM (Three Speed—Magical Maid IV.) White 7/1
4—Mr. John Wanamaker............bd.d. OLD BEAN (Wingle—Washover) ...... Green 2/1
5—Mrs. Reginald Foster ....br.d. AIR HAWK (Hawklike—Air Combat) .. Black 3/1
6—Mr. J. C. M. Kerslake ....bk.d. HAPPY ACCEPTANCE (Jasper—Happy Coming) Orange 10/1
7—Mrs. Marshall Roberts ....f.d. SUDBOURNE STIFF (Hawklike—Silvery Brook) Red & White 10/1

1st MISTLEY - 2nd OLD BEAN - 3rd SUDBOURNE STIFF
8¼ - HEAD   TIME 25:00

SECOND RACE

The Stanley Course (500 yds.)   7-55 p.m.
                                                              Colours.

1—Miss Mary Astor Paul ....f.d. MIGHTY (Happy Bertie—Molly XI.) .. Red 2/1
2—Miss Constance Talmadge ....r.d. PHILOSOPHER (Derringer—Fantasy) .... Blue 10/1
3—Mrs. J. C. King ....f.d. FAIRLY KEEN (Admiral's Echo—Wild Iris) White 5/1
4—Mrs. Marshall Roberts ....f.d. LOPEX (Admiral's Echo—Wild Iris) ...... Green 10/1
5—Mr. A. R. Tozer ....bd.b. AFTER TIME (Barr-na-Maidne—Lockspit Lady) Black 10/1
6—Mr. P. M. Stewart ....bd.d. BANNOCKBURN (Fine Fight—Air Combat) Orange 10/1
7—Lord Stanley ....bd.b. EMERALD BROOCH (Skeets—Vicious Ada) Red & White 3/1

1st BANNOCKBURN - 2nd MIGHTY - 3rd EMERALD BROOCH
1¼   3¼   TIME 28:80

They're off. Greyhound racing in the UK has a standard colour scheme. Trap 1: Red racing jacket with white numeral. Trap 2: Blue with white numeral. Trap 3: White with black numeral. Trap 4: Black with white numeral. Trap 5: Orange with black numeral. Trap 6: Black and white stripes with red numeral. Trap 7: Green with red numeral. Trap 8: Yellow and black with white numeral. A racing jacket worn by a reserve dog also carries the letter 'R' on each side.

(Opposite page top). The front cover of the programme from the first ever greyhound meeting in the UK and the runners for the first two races. Mistley, ironically the first dog listed, went on the win the first race, coming in at 6 to 1 with Bannockburn romping home at 10 to 1 in the second.

Emerald Brooch, owned by Lord Stanley, ran third in the second race. Emerald Brooch's father, Skeets, also sired Elder Brother who ran third in the first greyhound Derby. As with almost anything Belle Vue did, the meetings became world famous and very popular, attracting huge crowds.

Within a few years, greyhound racing gave us a new catchphrase. "Going to the dogs". It is said to have come about through workers blowing their week's pay on a visit to the local track. Gambling away the weekly pay packet before getting home was nothing new. My grandfather turned up skint on many an occasion having lost the lot playing shove ha'penny.

(Opposite page bottom). In 1876, an attempt was made at Hendon to turn hare coursing into more of a race meeting with a field of six greyhounds chasing a mechanical hare over a 400yd (366metre) straight course. It failed to catch on.

Step forward 43 years to 1919 and Emeryville, California. Owen Patrick Smith, an early advocate against cruelty in sport, came up with an alternative to using live jack rabbits for coursing. Smith developed the oval circuit, using a mechanical jack rabbit. The Emeryville track had stands for spectators similar to those at horse racecourses. It also led to the establishment of professional greyhound racing.

In 1926, Smith's concept came to the UK. American businessman Charles Mann and Canadian Major Lyne-Dixon teamed up with Brigadier-General Critchley and Sir William Gentle to form the International Greyhound Racing Association. On 24 July 1926, around 1,700 spectators watched the first greyhound meeting in the UK – at Belle Vue.

This opening meeting – one of the races is pictured here - featured fields of seven greyhounds chasing an electric-powered hare. In the early days of the sport, a slow hare was used in order to draw the greyhounds away from the inner rail as shown in this image. Today, most races are run with six dogs. The judges' box can be seen on the inside of the track.

(Above).The main stand at Belle Vue dog track. By the end of 1927, around 40 tracks had opened, including, White City, Harringay and Henlow. The first English greyhound Derby (over 500yds, 460metres) was run at White City on 15 October 1927, offering substantial prize money: £1,000 to the winner, £300 to the runner-up and £100 to the third place. In 2018 terms this equates to £58,200 for the winner, £17,460 for the runner-up and £5,820 for third place. Finalists were selected from northern and southern heats, and included the Belle Vue-trained greyhounds Banderloo and Great Chum. However, Great Chum was withdrawn due to illness and replaced in the final by Derham Boy.

(Middle). *MEN* photographer John Featherstone's image of the new stand taken on 29 April 1960. It cost £30,000 – just under £665,000 in 2018 prices.

In September 1976, racegoers could either stand outside or enjoy a meal.

reddie Garrity, of Freddie and the Dreamers, and singer Kathy Kirby enjoying an evening at Belle Vue dog track. The image is dated June 966 by which time both of their careers had peaked. Between mid-1963 and the end of 1964, Freddie and the Dreamers had achieved four op 10 UK hit singles and appeared in four movies. Between 1963 and 1965, Kathy Kirby had four Top 20 hit singles, two TOP 20 albums, epresented the UK in the 1965 *Eurovision Song Contest*, and made two series for TV. In October 1966, she would star in the BBC2 show *ternational Cabaret*.

The burnt-out Tote board following a fire in May 1980. In the UK, attendance peaked in 1946 when an estimated 70million people passed through the turnstiles. It began a steady decline following the opening of betting shops in 1961. Until then, off-course betting was illegal. However, it was possible to place an off-course bet – as a ten-year-old in the 1950s, I used to run my dad's bets for him. Punters would write their bets on a scrap of paper and sign it with a pseudonym – my dad's was Duke MM. In 1946, the on-course Tote betting generated £196.4million whereas in 2017 the on and off course Tote generated a combined total of £75million.

Over nearly a century of dog racing, there have been 143 regulated tracks and at least 256 unregulated ones. Now there are just 21 licenced and five independent tracks operating, attracting around two million punters a year.

Colin Delaney, Assistant General Manager of the greyhound stadium, with the plans for the new track.

Fever Maid and Silver Circle training at Belle Vue. Fever Maid was born in Ireland on 18 October 1993; her father was the 1992 Irish Derby winner Manx Treasure. Silver Circle was born in Ireland on 2 September 1994; his father, Slippy Blue, had won the 1989 Sussex Cup and the 1990 English Derby.

orman Johnson receives the 1993 Demmy Racing sponsored Northern Flat Championship trophy from the sponsor's managing director Ken ohnston. Dating back to 1927, the Northern Flat is one of the oldest competitions in the calendar. The first holder was the Belle Vue-trained reat Chum. In the 1932 race, Wild Woolley, trained at Belle Vue by Jimmy Campbell, set a track record for the distance; a record that stood r more than 50 years until broken by Precious Prince in 1984. To date, only two dogs have succeeded in winning the trophy back-to-back. lutable in 1928 and 1929, and Rushton Mac in 1954 and 1955.

reyhounds in action at Belle Vue, July 1995. As well as the Northern Flat, Belle Vue is the venue for the Scurry Gold Cup. Like the Northern at, this trophy race goes back to the early days of greyhound racing in the UK and was first run at Belle Vue in 2009. The Cock o' the North ophy race was inaugurated at the White City Stadium in 1960, and later relocated to Belle Vue, where the first winner was Decoy Dorothy.

The entrance to the speedway stadium. The initials are those of Manchester Central Football Club. The club was formed in 1928 by Manchester City director John Ayrton and John Iles in the belief that East Manchester needed its own professional League football club.

Central's first team played in the Lancashire Combination, the reserves in the Cheshire County League. An application to join the Football League for the 1929-30 season was rejected, and they lost out to Chester City with their application for 1930-31. Central withdrew from the Lancashire Combination for a first team place in the Cheshire County League.

In October 1931, Central were initially accepted to replace Wigan Borough in the Third Division (North) following Borough's resignation. However, both Manchester City and Manchester United objected and Central were refused. Central resigned from the Cheshire County League and the side was dissolved.

In 2015 a new Manchester Central was formed.

The legendary Manchester City, Manchester United, and Welsh international outside-right Billy Meredith was hired as Central's coach.

Big Daddy (on the left) alias Shirley Crabtree faces up to 6ft 11ins (211cm) tall Martin Ruane alias Giant Haystacks. The crowd loved Big Daddy. Playing the eternal good guy, he always approached the ring with great energy and usually made quick work of his opponents, finishing them off with his famous belly splash. The rivalry between Big Daddy and Giant Haystacks enthralled the nation for years, though they often formed a team when tag-wrestling became popular. As well as Giant Haystacks, Martin Ruane fought under other names including: Loch Ness Monster, Wayne Young and Little Haystacks. In November 1978, he beat Tony St Clair to take the British Heavyweight Title only for St Clair to win it back the following April. In Calgary, Canada, in February 1980, Loch Ness Monster defeated Joe Ventura and Tsutomu Oshiro in a two-on-one handicap. It is alleged that the first live televised bout between Big Daddy and Giant Haystacks drew an audience of 18 million.

Two-year-old David Edwards, of Park Street, Heaton Park, Manchester, looks up at 23-year-old 6ft 11ins (211cm) tall French wrestler Jean Ferre. Ferre used at least eight different names during his career including Andre the Giant and Monster Roussimoff. Jean Ferre was also one of them – his real name was in fact Andre Rene Roussimoff. Ferre's billed height was 7ft 4ins (224cm) with a billed weight of 520lb (236kg). Ferre was in the UK to wrestle. He had two matches in Manchester, defeating Rocky Wall on 26 July 1969 and then Pat Roache at Belle Vue on 4 October. He lost only one match during his tour – against Kendo Nagasaki at Hanley on 7 June.

(Below). Kendo Nagasaki (Peter Thornley) demonstrates a few moves on *Daily Mirror* journalist Murray Davies. Nagasaki was not the only wrestler to wear a mask. Count Bartelli (Geoff Condliffe) did so too. Bartelli went undefeated for 20 years until March 1966 when he fought Nagasaki at the Victoria Hall, Hanley, Stoke-on-Trent. The price of defeat was to be unmasked. In December 1976, the *TV Times* stated that Nagasaki had been voted the most popular and the most hated wrestler by fans at Belle Vue.

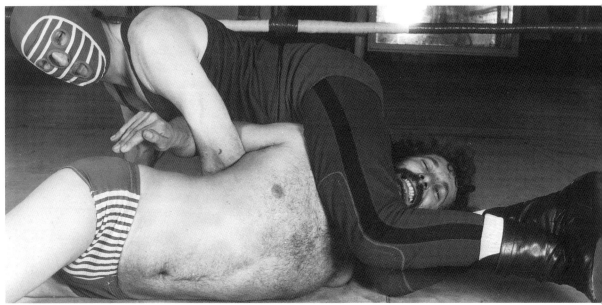

Born at Collyhurst in 1909, flyweight Jackie Brown was only 16 when, in May 1925, he had his first professional bout, defeating Harry Gaines on points. Four years later, Brown won the vacant British Boxing Board of Control (BBBofC) British Flyweight title by knocking out Bert Kirby in the third round. In March 1930, Kirby mounted a title challenge and this time it was he who won in the third round by knocking out Brown. In February 1931, the pair clashed for a third time, going the full 15 rounds for Brown to regain the title on points.

The Kings Hall was the venue for countless title fights. It was here on 9 September 1935, that Brown lost his BBBofC British Flyweight and National Boxing Association World Flyweight titles to Benny Lynch by a technical knockout, when the referee stopped the contest in the second round. Brown then tried his luck at bantamweight and on 5 October 1936, beat Len Hampstead on points to take the vacant BBBofC Northern Area title. The following year, Brown had a crack at the British title. On 31 May, he fought Johnny King at Belle Vue but was knocked out in the 13th round. Six months later he lost his Northern Area title to Len Hampstead.

Belle Vue was the venue for Brown's last fight before retiring. He beat Benny Jones on points. During his career, Brown had 140 professional fights, winning 107, losing 24 and drawing nine. He fought 40 times at Belle Vue, the first occasion being on 26 June 1929, when he defeated Jim Campbell by a technical knock out in the ninth of a twelve-round bout.

The Rochdale Thunderbolt, Jock McAvoy, knocks out Archie Sexton at Belle Vue on 9 October 1933, and retains his BBBofC British Middleweight and Commonwealth (British Empire) Middleweight titles. Belle Vue was where Jock fought in defence of his titles. On 24 June 1935, he defeated Al Bourke on points but ten months later, his luck ran out, losing his titles on points to Jack Petersen at Earls Court. However, Jock had not given up. On 27 April 1937, he knocked out Eddie Phillips to take the British Light Heavyweight title and six months later won back his Middleweight titles when he beat Jack Hyams by a technical knockout at Belle Vue. Jock's last defence of his titles at Belle Vue came on 22 May 1939, when he beat Arthur (Ginger) Sadd on points. His last non-title contest at Belle Vue was on 29 April 1940, when his opponent Jim Berry retired.

In 1947, Peter Kane and Theo Medina had two fights at Belle Vue. Our image is from their contest on 9 June, which Kane won when the Frenchman retired. On 19 September they met again, only this time the EBU European Bantamweight title was at stake. It was a win on points for Kane, as was his defence of his title just three months later, when he fought Joe Cornelis at Belle Vue. Belle Vue featured in the majority of Kane's remaining fights before he retired. It was here on 20 February 1948 that he lost his EBU title to Guido Ferracain, and fared no better in their rematch just five months later. Kane's last contest at Belle Vue was on 19 November 1948, when he lost on points to Stan Rowan. Our image shows Kane on the ropes in the second round.

Spaniard Boby Ros and South African Willie Toweel go to it on 6 September 1957. A talented flyweight, Toweel had won a bronze medal at the 1952 Olympics and the following year turned professional. On 11 March 1956, he fought 21-year-old Hubert Essakow at the City Hall, Johannesburg. It was during the 11th round that Toweel knocked his opponent out. Essakow never regained consciousness and died a few days later. The death haunted Toweel throughout his career to the extent that he would back off once his opponent had been hurt. Despite this, Toweel secured the South African and Commonwealth (British Empire) lightweight titles before coming to the UK in 1957 on a six-fight tour. Included was a defence of his Commonwealth (British Empire) title against Dave Charnley. By the time he faced Ros, Toweel had successfully defended his title, as well as beating Billy (Spider) Kelly on points. The contest against Ros also ended in a win on points as did those against Mario Calcaterra and Jimmy Carter. His last bout before returning to South Africa to face Al Nevarez, was against Jose Hernandez which Toweel won by a technical knockout.

Orthodox middleweight Terry Downes works out in his room at Manchester's Midland Hotel on 8 June 1960 in readiness for his fight the following evening at the Kings Hall against Richard Bouchez. Downes already held the British and Commonwealth middleweight titles, and this was his only fight between knocking out Orlando Di Pietro on 24 March and defending his British title against Phil Edwards on 5 July. Fans hoping the contest against Bouchez would go the whole ten rounds were soon disappointed when Downes knocked out his opponent in the second. Downes had two more fights at Belle Vue. On 25 November 1963, he beat Mike Pusateri on a technical knockout. The other contest turned out to be Downes' 44th, and last, professional appearance in the ring. On 30 November 1964, he faced Willie Pastrano for the World Boxing Association (WBA) and World Boxing Council (WBC) light heavyweight titles. Downes lost by a technical knockout. Our other image shows Downes with the Rochdale Thunderbolt, Jock McAvoy, holder of both the British and Commonwealth (British Empire) middleweight titles in the 1930s.

John (Cowboy) McCormack on the canvas after being knocked out in the sixth by George Aldridge during their contest for the vacant BBBofC British Middleweight Title at Belle Vue on 26 November 1962.

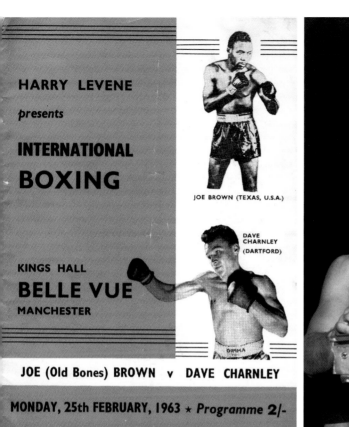

HARRY LEVENE

presents

INTERNATIONAL
BOXING

JOE BROWN (TEXAS, U.S.A.)

DAVE CHARNLEY (DARTFORD)

KINGS HALL
BELLE VUE
MANCHESTER

JOE (Old Bones) BROWN v DAVE CHARNLEY

MONDAY, 25th FEBRUARY, 1963 ★ Programme 2/-

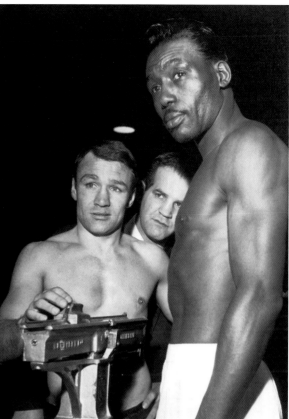

Dave Charnley checks the scales for Joe (Old Bones) Brown at the weigh-in at the Kings Hall for their ten-round super lightweight contest in February 1963. Charnley won by a technical knockout in the eighth round. It was to be three in a row at Belle Vue for Charnley. In May, he mounted a successful defence of his British lightweight title against Maurice Cullen and in November lost on points to Tito Marshall.

Dave Charnley, aged 27, training at Belle Vue for his fight against Maurice Cullen, aged 25. Charnley was defending his BBBofC Lightweight title in a 15-round contest. Southpaw Charnley had already had 56 professional fights, Cullen had fought professionally 28 times. Charnley emerged the clear winner on points.

Our Henry's only appearance at Belle Vue during his professional career was on 24 February 1964, in defence of his British and Commonwealth heavyweight titles as well as for the then vacant EBU European Heavyweight Title. His opponent was Brian London. This was the pair's third contest, having first met in 1956 in a non-title fight at Earl's Court, Empress Hall. Scheduled to last ten rounds, the fight ended in the first when Henry was declared the winner on a technical knockout. Their second contest came in January 1959, when London was defending his British and Commonwealth heavyweight titles. The bout went the full 15 rounds, Henry being awarded a win on points. Henry Cooper's claim to fame is that he was the only boxer to put the Louisville Lip, the one-and-only Muhammad Ali (Cassius Clay), on the canvas when he landed an upward angled left hook. during their non-title fight at Wembley in 1963.

British and Commonwealth heavyweight title contender Brian London is seen here losing on points to Henry Cooper at Belle Vue on 24 February 1964. London's first contest at Belle Vue was on 11 November 1955, when he knocked out Prosper Black in first round of what was supposed to be a ten-round fight. It would be seven years before London returned to Belle Vue, where he secured a win on points against Young Jack Johnson on 2 February 1962. London returned to Belle Vue on 5 February 1966, losing on points to Thad Spencer. Interestingly, both Henry Cooper's and Brian London's last professional fights were against Joe Bugner. Both lost.

Alan Rudkin celebrates regaining his BBBofC British Bantamweight Title with a win over Evan Armstrong at Belle Vue on 9 June 1969. A regular visitor to Manchester, Rudkin's first contest at Belle Vue was an eight-round bout against Brian Bissmire on 20 May 1963. Rudkin won in the seventh when Bissmire was disqualified. By the time Rudkin returned to the Kings Hall to fight Baby John on 30 November 1964, he had defeated Pierre Vetroff, Danny Lee, Don Weller and Orizu Obilaso as well as beating Brian Cartwright no less than three times. Rudkin did not return to Belle Vue until 1966, winning both contests; Edmundo Esparza (31 Jan) and Jose Bisbel (24 Oct) on points. His next contest at Belle Vue was the big one; against Walter McGowan for both the British and Commonwealth bantamweight titles. The Kings Hall was packed to the rafters with fight fans. At times there was little to choose between the contestants as they battled it out, though in the end the result went to Rudkin by 73.5 to 73 points. Only ten months later, Rudkin lost his Commonwealth title to Lionel Rose in Melbourne, Australia. Had he won, Rudkin would also have taken the WBC and WBA bantamweight titles. Our image was taken at his last contest at Belle Vue. On 9 June 1969, he fended off challenger Evan Armstrong to hold on to his BBBofC British Bantamweight Title.

Despite having a career that spanned 83 professional fights, orthodox heavyweight Joe Bugner fought only once at Belle Vue. On 9 June 1969, on the same bill as the Alan Rudkin vs Evan Armstrong contest, Bugner fought Moses Harrell in an eight-round non-title bout. Bugner won on points.

The one and only Mohammad Ali is ushered through a large crowd at the *MEN* Ideal Homes Exhibition staged at Belle Vue.

Mohammad Ali with local boxers Jonjo Greene and Alex Penarski. Greene was a light heavyweight who had 44 professional fights, 11 of which were fought in Manchester. He had five bouts at the Kings Hall, one apiece against Trevor Catthouse, Tom Collins and Alex Penarski and two against Bernie Kavanagh. Of these, he lost by a technical knockout to Tom Collins when the referee stopped the bout in the seventh due to Greene having a cut to the eye. Of his other Manchester bouts, Greene fought Antonio Harris at Stage One, on 15 November 1984, in an eliminator for the BBBofC British Light Heavyweight Title. He lost on points.

Jonjo Greene and cruiserweight Alex Penarski fought one another at the Kings Hall on 16 May 1983. Greene won on points.

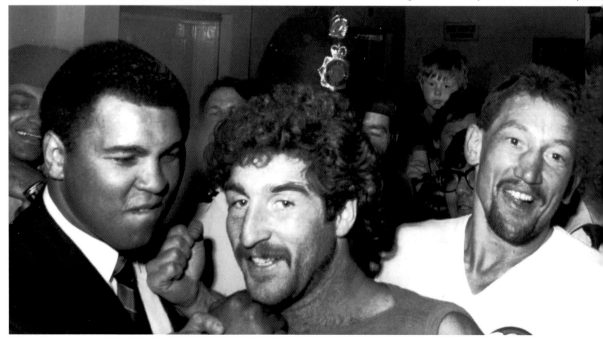

By the early 1950s, table tennis was attracting ever larger audiences and Belle Vue was expected to be packed to capacity for the 1953 English Open: the finals being on Friday, 13 November. It was anticipated that top European players such as Vilim Harangozo and the up-and-coming Conrad 'Conny' Freundorfer would make it a competition to remember. *The Manchester Evening News* table tennis columnist, Harold Evans, wrote about the sport's public following, and that audiences would not be fobbed off with half-hearted displays such as those witnessed the previous year when some of the best players in the world met the top British players at the Free Trade Hall. Our image shows 'Conny' Freundorfer during a practice match.

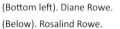

(Bottom left). Diane Rowe.

(Below). Rosalind Rowe.

Belle Vue table tennis finals, March 1956. Diane Rowe holds the Victor Barna player of the year trophy. Left handed Diane often teamed up with her twin sister Rosalind to play doubles games. The trophy was named after the great Hungarian table tennis player Victor Barna – the five times world singles champion who is credited for turning the game into a major sport.

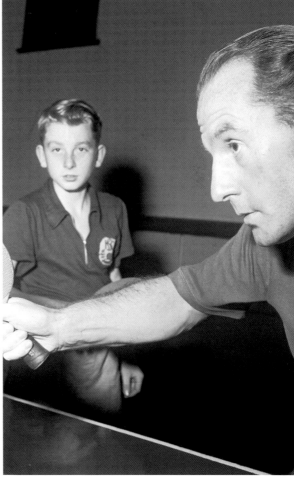

Ken Stanley, former England table tennis international, and his son David (12) practise for the 1957 North of England table tennis championships, where they had entered the men's doubles. Held 10-12 October 1957, David House and Joyce Fielder won the singles titles. It was Fielder's first major singles title. She also partnered Coilin Deaton to win the mixed doubles title. The men's doubles were won by P Strutavitch and J Ingber, who beat C Pullar and B Castotsky, 23-21 and 21-18.

Decline & Fall

By the late 1960s, car ownership was increasing and people were travelling farther afield for their entertainment. Though Belle Vue remained a popular place for pop and rock concerts, brass band competitions and conferences, visitor numbers declined - and Forte appeared unwilling to invest in the zoo and amusement park.

From 1966, traditional zoos like Belle Vue faced a new threat when the Marquess of Bath opened the first drive-through safari park outside Africa at his Longleat estate. Admission was set at £1 per car and five shillings each for coach passengers. On the first day, the vehicle queue waiting to enter the park stretched for four miles. During its first year, Longleat attracted an estimated 486,500 people, 106,000 cars and 1,950 coaches. The main attraction were the lions which were viewed from the safety of cars or coaches. Then, two years later, Longleat caused a sensation when it opened its game reserve. For the first time in the UK, visitors could walk and picnic amid giraffes and zebras.

Other safari and wildlife parks soon followed. Among them were the Cotswold Wildlife Park and Woburn Safari Park, both of which opened during 1970. Knowsley Safari Park followed in 1971 and the West Midland Safari Park in 1973.

In 1971, Peter Grayson was appointed as the new superintendent at Belle Vue Zoo. He would be the last. The zoo enjoyed a brief renaissance during the 1975 and 1976 seasons, but economic pressures and the unwillingness of Forte to invest took their toll. Costs were escalating and despite the best efforts of Grayson and a dedicated band of keepers, the zoo began to look tired, dilapidated, worn out. The zoo was losing £100,000 a year and its owners were not willing to take the hit.

At 9.00am on 4 August 1977, the 24 keepers were informed that the zoo would close on 11 September. An hour later the closure was announced on BBC Radio. New homes were found for most of the animals - some even found homes with their former keepers. The last animal at the zoo was Ellie May the elephant. Belle Vue had problems placing her but eventually, in February 1979, a new home was secured, and preparations were made for Ellie May to leave.

However, Ellie May refused to enter her transport and became distressed. It was decided that another attempt would be made the following day, but overnight she developed pneumonia and a serious heart complaint. Eventually, staff realised that it would be better for her to be put down. Ellie May died where she had lived, the last of the Belle Vue animals.

The rest of Belle Vue died by the death of a thousand cuts. In 1969, following criticism from Raymond Legge that some of the zoo's animals were suffering, the last fireworks display was held. Two years later one of the attraction's iconic landmarks – the Bobs - was demolished, as maintenance and upkeep costs were considered too high. With no injection of cash, rides closed as costs rose. What was left of the amusement park was eventually rented out to a Mr Wadbrooke, but openings were restricted to weekends, holidays and bank holidays.

The agreement with Wadbrooke came to an end following negotiations between Trust House Forte and the City planners as to what to do with the site. It was agreed Belle Vue would be sacrificed and, in its place, developers would build a mixture of housing and light industry. The site was sold in January 1981 to the Espley Tyas Development Group, though Forte struck a deal whereby the new owners would honour outstanding commitments for 18 months – including the 1981-82 Christmas Circus. Excluded from the sale were the Speedway Stadium, though it was later sold to Stuart Bamforth. The Bowling Centre was also excluded from the sale and eventually passed into the hands of the First Leisure Corporation after they acquired Trust House Forte's leisure portfolio.

There followed a wave of protests. Fifty thousand people signed a petition in an attempt to block the sale. Some of the protesters even formed their own development company that devised a new scheme more in keeping with Belle Vue's original usage. It was no use, the sale to Espley Tyas went through and during September 1981 much of the site was demolished, though the speedway stadium and the bowling centre were saved.

The last music event staged in the Kings Hall was the North West Amateur Brass Band Championship in February 1982.

No less than 56 bands and 1,700 musicians took part in a venue that should have already been in the hands of the demolition men. However, a fire at the final's intended venue – Bolton Town Hall – earned the Kings Hall a brief stay of execution when owners Espley Tyas agreed to postpone demolition for two weeks.

In 1983, the Exhibition Halls were taken over by Mullet Ltd, who had some initial success in reviving this part of Belle Vue. But the opening of G-Mex in 1986 was a hammer blow and was directly responsible for the site being sold on to the British Car Auctions Group, who demolished the remaining buildings and replaced them with a large car auction centre.

The gates had well and truly closed on Belle Vue, though for some, even now nearly 40 years later, the memories linger on. What was once a place of fun, entertainment and education, has become an anonymous residential and industrial area that many would not take a second look at. It seems impossible that here on Manchester's doorstep there once existed a place where as many as 150,000 people a day would visit, to see animals from the far corners of the earth, to eat and drink, to dance in the sumptuous surroundings of the ballroom, listen to music in the Kings Hall, ride the roller coasters, watch sport and experience the sights, sounds and smells of its legendary circus.

Laurence Baker had worked for 40 years as a keeper. He is pictured saying goodbye to the big cats he cared for as news of the zoo's closure is confirmed.

Despite a good summer, by November 1976 the costs associated with operating the zoo were escalating and the owners were unwilling to invest. These Cheshire children schoolchildren – pictured with head keeper John Christy – won a free visit to the zoo after collecting 50 tons of waste paper that would be made into shredbeds for the animals.

This image just about says it all. Selling the animals was a relatively slow process, some being easier to place than others. Many animals went to Cleethorpes whilst Bristol Zoo bought the pygmy hippos and the gorillas. The orangutans went to a private collection at Wadebridge. Twiggy the elephant went to a zoo in the Netherlands. Some of the smaller mammals and reptiles even found homes with former keepers.

Matt Kelly, retired Head Keeper, returned to Belle Vue to protest against the demolition of the site. Despite the efforts on his and many other people's part, the decline of the zoo proved unstoppable and the site was levelled. (Below). Matt Kelly with members of the Belle Vue action group outside Manchester Town Hall.

Jacko Fossett without his clown apparel sitting in the Kings Hall for the last time before it was demolished. Although the circus would continue for a few more seasons, it would no longer be performed within the famous hall.

Before the closure of the last circus Christmas Circus to be staged in the Kings Hall, a circus christening service was performed by the Rev Anthony Carr.

It was left to the Glossop School Band to play the last piece of music to be heard in the Kings Hall. Demolition of the building had been put on hold so that the 1982 North West Amateur Brass Band Championship could be staged there. The winners were Dobcross Band.

(Opposite page top). Panels from the Belle Vue Wall of Fame, seen here after been retrieved during the demolition of the Elizabethan Suite. Among the names of stars from the past are: actor Omar Sharif and singers Bing Crosby and Gracie Fields.

(Opposite page bottom). The wooden structure, once the home of the Belle Vue Circus, wrestling and boxing matches and brass band competitions, is no more. This rubble-strewn site is where the Kings Hall once stood. When the site was being redeveloped for housing, the bones of several long-dead animals were discovered, including a giraffe. It is thought the bones dated back to Jennison days.

Acknowledgements

Heather Stackhouse and Daniel Hyams' original 2005 text forms the basis of this new edition, so along with them, I wish to acknowledge the following organisations and individuals.

Jan Hollins and her father James for granting access to their family photographs. To Tommy Kelly for not only the use of some of the images in his collection but fascinating background information on the zoo in general and his father Matt in particular. Also, Tommy, many thanks for reading through the second edition text.

Special thanks go to David Gray at The Monastery of St Francis and Gorton Trust, for not only sharing his memories with Heather and Daniel but also volunteering to read through the second edition to make sure there were no inaccuracies.

Also, thanks to Jane Foster at Chethams Library and the staff at Manchester Central Library's Local History Department for their invaluable help and assistance.

Heather, Daniel and I, acknowledge the research and writings of Clive Bennett, David Barnaby, Frank Rhodes, Jill Cronin, C H Keeling, Robert Nicholls, Trevor James and Barry Stevenson.

We also wish to thank photographers and journalists of the *Manchester Evening News* and *Daily Mirror* including: Ian Currie, John Holland, John Featherstone, Bill Batchelor, Tony Cordt, Clive Cooksey, John Fowler, Eric Graham, Mike Grimes, Arthur Bottomley, David Burke, Harold Evans, Monte Fresco, Tommy Lea, Peter Price, Charlie Ley, Howard Walker, Tom Lyons, Alfred Markey and David Salt.

Also, thanks to John Mead and Simon Flavin at Mirrorpix.

Finally, as with the first edition, I hope this book allows visitors and former workers alike to share in a few memories of what was once Manchester's most magical of places. Though the place itself is now consigned to history, the memories will linger on for a few more years.

Clive Hardy.

2018.